Fit for Work

The Complete Guide to Managing
Sickness Absence and Rehabilitation

Fit for Work

The Complete Guide to Managing
Sickness Absence and Rehabilitation

an **eef** guide

Reissued in 2005 by
EEF
Broadway House
Tothill Street
London SW1H 9NQ
www.eef.org.uk

In association with Profile Books Ltd
www.profilebooks.com

Fit for Work was first published by EEF in 2004

10 9 8 7 6 5 4 3 2 1

Text design by Sue Lamble
Typeset in FS Albert by MacGuru Ltd
info@macguru.org.uk

Printed and bound in Great Britain by Bell & Bain Ltd, Glasgow

A CIP catalogue record for this book is available from the British Library.

ISBN 1 903461 71 5

Disclaimer

This publication represents our understanding of the law as at January 2004. It is intended to provide general guidance only. The publication is not intended to replace the need to obtain proper advice in relation to any matter discussed. EEF is not responsible for any acts or omissions arising from the use of this publication. More detailed advice on particular issues is available through your EEF Association.

Contents

Foreword   xiii

Fit for work: The strategy   1

Introduction   1
A six-step strategy   2
Step 1 – Clearly define roles within the company   2
Step 2 – Identify priorities for action   3
Step 3 – Involve and inform the workforce   4
Step 4 – Establish ready access to occupational health support   4
Step 5 – Focus on rehabilitation   5
Step 6 – Tackle frequent short-term absence   6
Importance of training   6
Practical assistance from EEF Associations   7
What is next in this Guide?   7
Case study 1: an EEF member company that reduced its absence level
from 9 % to less than 2 % in under a year   7

Legal overview   15

Introduction   15
Overlap between the Disability Discrimination Act and rehabilitation   16
    Is rehabilitation ever a legal requirement?   16
    Managing long-term absence against the backdrop of the DDA   17
    Who is protected under the DDA?   17
    What amounts to prohibited discrimination?   17
    Code of Practice   18
    What amounts to less favourable treatment?   18
    What is the duty to make reasonable adjustments?   19
    What is the test for justifying less favourable treatment?   19
The duty to make reasonable adjustments in more depth   20
    To whom is the duty to make reasonable adjustments owed?   21
    Does the DDA suggest what adjustments we should consider?   21
    What is a 'reasonable' adjustment?   23
    Can an employer justify failing to make an adjustment?   24
Health and safety requirements when employing people with disabilities   24

Unfair dismissal	24
General principles	24
Dismissals for frequent short-term absenteeism	25
Frustration of contract	26
Pregnancy-related absence	27
Introduction of statutory procedural rules from 1 October 2004	27
Purpose	27
To what kind of employment disputes do the statutory procedural rules apply?	28
What do the statutory procedures require employers to do?	29
Which employees are covered by the new procedural rules?	29
What are the penalties for the employer of not following the statutory procedural rules?	30
Importance of keeping records of action taken prior to dismissal	31
Statutory right to be accompanied	31
Summary of employees' entitlements on dismissal	31

Step 1: Clearly define roles within the company	33
Introduction	33
Leading the strategy – the role of senior managers	34
Key elements of senior management's role	35
What aspects of attendance management should line managers be responsible for?	36
Personnel support	37
Companies without a formal personnel function	38
Health and safety representatives	39

Step 2: Identify priorities for action	40
What are the key questions a company needs to answer?	40
How to answer these questions	41
Calculating the cost of absence	41
Why calculate the cost?	41
Risk assessments	42
Monitoring absence	43
Why monitor absence?	43
Distinction between monitoring 'absence' and 'health' information	43
Recording absence information	44
Who should make the records?	44
Fair and lawful processing of absence information	44
Analysing attendance records	45
Introduction	45
Main management tools and their purpose	45
Severity	46

Frequency   46
Analysing the length of absence   46
The Bradford score   47
Monitoring employees' health   48
Why do it?   48
How to do it   48
Handling health information   50
Occupational health professionals' duty of medical confidentiality   50
Employees' rights to control access to their health information   51
Fair and lawful processing of health information under the
Data Protection Act   52
General obligations   52
Storing health information   54
Can an employee see what health information we hold about them?   54
The employer's implied duty of trust and confidence   54
The employee's right to privacy under the Human Rights Act – does it
prevent employers from conducting surveillance of employees
who are off sick?   54

Step 3: Involve and inform the workforce   56

Introduction   56
Informing employees already on long-term sickness absence of any
new initiatives   57
Induction   57
Legal obligation to inform employees in writing of rules and procedures
dealing with attendance   59
A written attendance management policy   59
Informing individual employees of the policy and making changes to it   60

Step 4: Establish ready access to occupational health support   61

How can we benefit from improved access to occupational health support?   61
How can occupational health advisers support us?   61
Reducing general risks to health within the workplace   62
Reducing absence in relation to particular individuals   62
Deciding on a level of occupational health support   64
Where do we obtain good quality occupational health support?   65
Rehabilitation: what Government assistance is available?   66
Disability Employment Advisers   66
Access to Work Scheme   66
Workstep   67
New Deal for Disabled People   67
WorkCare   68
Further contacts   68

Step 5: Focus on rehabilitation | 70

Introduction | 70
What is rehabilitation? | 70
The business case for rehabilitation | 70
Isn't it simpler for the employee to stay off sick? | 71
Benefits of early intervention | 72
Wouldn't we just be opening the floodgates to unmanageable requests
for special treatment? | 72
Wouldn't rehabilitation just increase pressure on colleagues? | 73
Wouldn't colleagues just see rehabilitation as unfair special treatment? | 74
Rehabilitation in practice | 74
Case management | 75
Adopting a flexible case management approach | 75
Flow chart – handling medical cases: a line manager's guide | 76
What is a case management approach? | 79
Making a case management approach work successfully | 79
When to start the rehabilitation process | 80
Maintaining contact with employees from the start of an absence | 80
Wouldn't contacting the sick employee be seen as harassment? | 81
When to actively consider rehabilitation | 82
Consultation with employee about rehabilitation | 83
Asking the right questions of the employee | 84
If we ask too many questions, the company might find out the employee
has a disability. Isn't this unwise? | 85
Next steps | 85
Typical rehabilitation measures | 86
Introduction | 86
Encourage visits to the workplace to 'keep in touch' | 87
Allow a phased return to work | 87
Alter the pattern of work | 87
Alter the employee's tasks or work content | 88
Adapt the workplace | 88
Reduce the pace of work | 88
Adapt tools and equipment | 88
Provide further training or information | 89
Provide for mobility and transport | 89
Further reading: 'Line managers' resource pack' for managing mental
health in the workplace | 90
Paying for treatment | 90
Should a business pay for treatment or medical investigations? | 90
Is payment always in the company's and employee's best interests? | 91
Ensuring employees are treated equitably when considering
paying for treatment | 92

Tax liability | 92
Obtaining medical information | 93
Consent to provide medical information | 93
Can we force an employee to attend an interview with our
own medical advisers? | 93
Can we withhold sick pay if an employee refuses consent to attend
the company's doctor? | 94
Contacting the employee's GP/specialist | 95
How do we ensure the company receives good quality medical information? | 95
Checklist: what should we include in a request for medical information? | 96
When should we ask for the GP's opinion on when the employee will be
fit to return to the original job? | 98
Should we now ask the GP's view on whether the employee qualifies under
the DDA? | 98
Deciding what the company should do next | 99
Assessing all the medical information received | 99
What if conflicting medical evidence is received? | 99
What are the implications of the medical evidence? | 100
Importance of further consultation with the employee | 100
Managing a rehabilitation programme | 101
Properly document the terms of the rehabilitation arrangements | 101
Monitoring the employee's progress and preventing relapses | 102
Can rehabilitation impede an employee's recovery? | 103
Stick to review dates | 103
Carry out health and safety risk assessments for the adjusted role | 104
What if rehabilitation is not appropriate or fails? | 104
General principles | 104
Summary of legal obligations | 105
Checking that the employer has complied with the DDA | 106
Ensuring the employer warns employees that dismissal may be an
outcome and complying with the statutory disciplinary and dismissal
and grievance procedures | 106
Ensuring the company has sufficient medical evidence | 107
Deciding on dismissal | 108
Contractual ill-health benefits | 109
Ill-health early retirement | 109
Employee who suffers a catastrophic illness | 111
Overcoming barriers to rehabilitation | 111
Poor access to occupational health advice | 112
Reluctant managers | 112
Reasons for reluctance | 112
Isn't rehabilitation too much effort? | 112
Isn't rehabilitation too complicated? | 113
Doesn't rehabilitation just result in more DDA-protected employees
on the company's headcount? | 113

Medical certificates and GPs   115
    The issues   115
    The sick note culture   115
    GPs signing employees off for longer than is medically necessary   117
    Vague medical certificates   119
    Referral to an occupational health adviser   119
    Can we withhold sick pay if we receive a vague medical certificate?   120
        SSP   120
        Government assistance for establishing entitlement to SSP   120
        Company sick pay   121
Dealing with reluctant employees   122
    The issues   122
    Ask occupational health adviser to contact GP   123
    Can we withhold sick pay if the employee refuses to co-operate with a
    rehabilitation programme?   124
        SSP   124
        Company sick pay   124
    Can we dismiss a reluctant employee?   126
    What if there is a conflict of opinion between the occupational health
    adviser and the GP about the scope for rehabilitation?   127
    Pay and job protection   127
    Employees with work-related personal injury claims   129
NHS delays   130
Integrating rehabilitation into existing arrangements for managing
long-term ill-health   130
    Does a greater focus on rehabilitation mean we should abandon our
    existing policy for handling long-term absence?   130
    Can we unilaterally change our existing procedure for managing attendance?   130
    Wouldn't the unions see a focus on rehabilitation as a means of cutting
    down on sick pay entitlement?   131
    Checklist for an effective attendance management policy emphasising
    rehabilitation   132
Case studies   134
    Case study 2 – managing an employee with lower back pain   134
    Case study 3 – managing an employee with stress   136
    Case study 4 – how should we handle an employee who goes off sick during
    disciplinary proceedings?   142

Step 6: Tackle frequent short-term absence   145

Introduction   145
Causes of short-term absence   145
Eradicating unnecessary short-term absence – what works and why?   146
How soon can companies expect improvements?   147

List of management tools considered in this Guide for tackling frequent
short-term absence 148
Formal action/disciplinary action 148
What type of formal action? 149
Should we treat poor attendance as a disciplinary issue? 149
Is there an alternative non-disciplinary approach? 150
Interrelationship between return to work interviews and formal action to
manage those employees with a poor attendance record 151
Reasons to keep separate the return to work interview from meetings for
formal action against poor attendees 151
Wilful misconduct 153
When to take formal action on the grounds of poor attendance 153
Overview 153
Ensuring consistency of treatment 154
What kind of trigger – comparative or absolute? 155
Keeping triggers under review 155
Do clearly defined triggers make dismissals on grounds of frequent
short-term absence safe? 155
**Should all short-term absences be counted when deciding whether to take
formal action to manage the employee's absence record?** 157
Absences which should always be excluded 157
Treatment of disability-related absences 157
Are there any other adjustments the employer should make for
disability-related absences? 159
When should we seek medical advice in cases of frequent short-term absence? 159
What procedural formalities should the company observe? 160
Overview 160
To what type of formal action connected with sickness absence do the
statutory minimum procedural rules apply (from 1 October 2004)? 161
Statutory right to be accompanied 163
Rigorous notification procedures 164
Objectives 164
Importance of clear rules 165
How can notification rules reduce frequent short-term absence? 165
Meeting these objectives 165
First contact 165
Subsequent contact 166
How should we treat an employee who goes 'AWOL'? 166
Return to work interviews 168
Introduction 168
Why are return to work interviews effective? 169
Establishing if the employee is fit enough to return to work 169
Asking what the problem is and respecting the employee's rights to
medical confidentiality 170

How should we respond if the employee reveals an underlying cause?   171
Link with harassment or dignity at work procedure   173
Taking further steps after a return to work interview   173
Conducting the return to work interview   174
Do's and Don'ts of a return to work interview   175
Training and support for managers in conducting return to work interviews   177
EEF training   178
Spot checks at an employee's home   178
Pre-employment screening   178
Controls in sick pay schemes   179
General principles   179
Requiring a doctor's certificate for all sickness absences, irrespective
of length   181
Inducements   183
'Good attendance' letters   183
Attendance bonuses   183
Can we reduce the holiday entitlement of employees with a poor
attendance record?   184
Team competition and absence 'league tables'   184
Making attendance count in employment decisions   185
Flexible working   186
Employee health initiatives   186

Appendix 1
Further detail of employees' rights on dismissal

Further detail of employees' rights on dismissal   189
Right of appeal   189
Hearing the appeal   190
Pay during notice period   190
Pay in lieu of notice   190
Other contractual rights   191
Written reasons for dismissal   191

Appendix 2
A hypothetical example using tools for analysing attendance records

A hypothetical example using tools for analysing
attendance records   192

About EEF   195
Index   198

Foreword

For UK manufacturers, competitive pressures have been consistently tight for so many years now that nearly every aspect of running a business is under the spotlight. Against this background, maximising attendance of employees has become a key performance indicator.

Simultaneously, employers are grappling with increasingly complex employment legislation including the Disability Discrimination Act 1995. There is also the threat of personal injury litigation, including work-related stress claims. With this comes the escalating cost of employer's liability insurance. These are pushing management of attendance, concern for employees' wellbeing, improving employees' rehabilitation prospects and establishing a strong safety culture to the top of the HR agenda.

A fresh approach

EEF believes the time is ripe for a new approach to dealing with these overlapping issues, one that fosters a climate of good attendance and a strong rehabilitation and health and safety culture.

We set out in this Guide the six elements of a strategy which are central to these goals. They can be tailored to meet the needs of companies of any size including those without a personnel function. This approach can help companies raise morale, productivity and efficiency and at the same time comply with the law. They can also meet the increasing standards being demanded by insurance companies.

Written primarily by a solicitor and an occupational physician employed by EEF, this Guide draws on the collective experience of EEF member companies and our Association officials and we would like to take this opportunity to thank all of those who participated directly and indirectly in its production.

Martin Temple

EEF Director-General

Fit for work: The strategy

Introduction

Without a doubt, maximising attendance of employees has become a key performance indicator. Simultaneously, employers are grappling with increasingly complex employment legislation. From 1 October 2004, the cost of making basic procedural mistakes in employment disputes may increase by as much as 50% (see pages 27–31). Many employers are also finding it difficult to manage employees on long-term ill-health absence against the backdrop of disability discrimination legislation. There is also the ever-present threat of personal injury litigation including work-related stress claims. With this comes the escalating cost of employer's liability insurance. There is also a significant gap between some employers' practices and what is required to minimise the threat of work-related personal injury cases, particularly stress-induced ones.

Generally speaking, the longer an employee is off work, the less likely he or she is to return to work. Leaving aside the misery this implies for individuals, this represents a significant loss to companies in skills training, experience and wasted recruitment costs. For those companies running occupational pension schemes, these figures translate into possibly avoidable ill-health early retirements which add to the financial burden of these schemes.

All of these issues are pushing management of attendance, improving employees' rehabilitation prospects and establishing a strong safety culture to the top of the HR agenda.

A six-step strategy

We set out in this Guide the six elements of a strategy which are central to these goals. Also, at a regional, national and European level, EEF is involved in many initiatives with the same objectives. In turn, these reflect the core aims of the Health and Safety Commission's ten-year strategy (2000–2010):

- to stop people being made ill by work

- to help people who are or have been ill or injured to return to work, and

- to improve work opportunities for people currently not in work due to ill health.

This Guide is primarily concerned with the second aim and specifically getting those who are already in employment back to work or, if still in work, working more effectively. There are two aspects to this, managing both short-term and long-term sickness absence, although there is often a great deal of overlap between the two. The steps we suggest have a real impact on managing these and they can be adapted to cover all types of company. They are:

Step 1 – Clearly define roles within the company

Step 2 – Identify priorities for action

Step 3 – Inform and involve the workforce

Step 4 – Establish ready access to occupational health support

Step 5 – Focus on rehabilitation, and

Step 6 – Tackle frequent short-term absence

These steps are summarised briefly below and then dealt with in detail in the corresponding chapters. We have also included at the end of this chapter (page 7) a case study of the experience of one of our member companies that has reduced its absence levels significantly by following these steps.

Step 1 – Clearly define roles within the company

Organisations differ depending on their size, sector, culture, unionised status etc, but, in EEF's experience, companies have the best odds for maximising attendance, improving employees' rehabilitation prospects and establishing a strong safety culture where:

- Senior managers take primary overall responsibility for developing and ensuring implementation of a strategy for meeting these goals and the workforce is left in no doubt that this is a senior management-led initiative and a priority for action.

- Line managers, rather than the personnel function, have the key day-to-day responsibility for managing attendance issues, for example, conducting return to work interviews.

- Line managers are trained to perform their roles, which includes helping them develop an awareness of 'medical incapacity' and the business reasons for the measures set out in this Guide.

- The company has ready access to occupational health support (see Step 4 for further details).

Where there is a personnel function they support senior and line managers in this programme. By monitoring they can check that line managers are adhering to guidelines and so ensure employees are treated consistently thereby reducing the risk of successful litigation. In smaller companies without a personnel function, the same controls can be assigned to a member of senior management.

On pages 33–9 we make recommendations for allocating responsibilities for various elements of the strategy set out in this Guide.

Step 2 – Identify priorities for action

Whilst longer spells of absence incur higher costs, companies often focus more on short-term absence when considering priorities for action. The reasons for this are mixed. Short-term absence is often more disruptive on a day-to-day basis but, even though long-term absence is more costly, it is not prioritised because managers often feel disempowered from tackling it.

In our view, companies should adopt a more balanced approach and identify priorities for action for both types of sickness absence. First, though, they must be able to record and measure absence properly. Simple management tools exist for this. These are set out on pages 45–8.

Companies must also diligently carry out risk assessments, not only for physical hazards and processes but all areas of employee health and safety, including stress-related conditions (see page 42). These too help employers identify priorities for action. A strategy for maximising attendance, improving employees' rehabilitation prospects and establishing a strong safety culture requires, therefore, co-ordination between those managers responsible for health and safety, including those carrying out risk assessments, occupational health professionals, personnel and operational managers.

Step 3 – Involve and inform the workforce

If a company resolves to have a major push to maximise attendance it needs to inform and involve its workforce. This is considered in more detail on pages 56–60.

Step 4 – Establish ready access to occupational health support

As will become clear from this Guide, a successful strategy for maximising attendance and improving employees' prospects for rehabilitation (thereby cutting down the level of unnecessary sickness absence and the number of dismissals and ill-health early retirements) depends on improved access to occupational health advice. Also, employers who use occupational health services routinely are much more likely to meet their obligations under relevant employment law, particularly if their advisers are involved early, are asked the right questions and given the right information.

It takes time, though, to set up access to occupational health advice and many SMEs, in particular, do not have established arrangements for obtaining it. Often, advice is only sought, if at all, in the very late stages of a long-term absence when the chances of successful rehabilitation may be reduced.

Unfortunately, in the UK, there is no national network of occupational health services and private provision is highly fragmented and of varying quality. In Step 4 we summarise how companies can ensure they have ready access to effective occupational health advice and explain what sources of state aid are available for rehabilitation.

Step 5 – Focus on rehabilitation

A key element in a strategy for maximising attendance is shifting the company from a passive response in cases of long-term absence to a culture of proactively managing each case, on its own facts, and with a strong focus on rehabilitation.

In many companies, it is still the case that an employee can be off sick for quite some time before any action is taken to review their status and often the main focus is whether the company should start a procedure for dismissing on the grounds of ill health. Typically these reviews occur when:

- the length of the employee's absence triggers a review under an absence control policy

- the employee's entitlement to sick pay is exhausted (this is particularly the case in companies with generous sick pay schemes)

- there are personnel changes, such as a new manager or a change in HR personnel – it is often then that an employee absent on long-term sick comes up on the radar, or

- organisational change is in the air, be it redundancy or other restructuring, or a possible merger/acquisition, which prompts management to look at staffing levels.

In contrast, where rehabilitation is central to managing long-term absence, management is actively involved in appropriate cases and at a much earlier stage than is often the case presently.

This is quite a cultural shift for many businesses, as many employees and employers perceive employees under a medical certificate to be 'untouchable'. Remember: an employer that focuses on rehabilitation is not challenging or questioning the validity of the medical certificate but, rather, shows willingness to look at temporary modifications to an employee's job to allow a return to some work or facilitate a return to work earlier than otherwise.

There can be long-term gains for both employers and employees and the process becomes easier as a business gains experience in rehabilitation (see also the case study on page 7). However, when temporary modifications are made it is important to monitor the employee's progress, document changes and keep the arrangements under review. All of these and other practical issues are dealt with in Step 5.

Step 6 – Tackle frequent short-term absence

This step involves rigorous use of tried and tested methods of tackling short-term absence, particularly 'return to work' interviews, clarifying and enforcing notification procedures, and, crucially, training managers how to use these methods effectively.

The objective should not be to punish those with legitimate reasons for being absent, but rather to create a climate in which attending work regularly becomes the norm and those who are frequently absent from work, or absent without good cause, are accountable for their record.

Importance of training

We cannot emphasise enough how important it is that a company buttresses its initiatives for managing attendance with adequate training. Many companies risk losing unfair dismissal and disability discrimination cases because they have not ensured that the line managers with operational responsibility for implementing a procedure or policy fully understand what is required of them, not just under general employment law but also under their employer's own procedures.

The need for this training will become more important when, from 1 October 2004, employers will be required to follow mandatory procedural rules or risk automatically unfair dismissal claims and increases in compensation awards (see pages 27–31). These penalties apply as much to dismissals on grounds of medical incapacity/frequent short-term absenteeism as dismissals for misconduct.

Practical assistance from EEF Associations

All companies, irrespective of their size or resources, even those without a dedicated personnel function, can benefit from the measures set out in this Guide if, with their EEF advisers, they assess what they can do themselves and identify where they may need extra support from EEF.

Many member companies have already benefited from the practical assistance EEF Associations can provide on all aspects of the strategy set out in the following pages. We suggest readers contact their EEF Association for further details of these services, including:

- reviewing existing practices and arrangements

- developing a new strategy

- training of line managers (including how to conduct return to work interviews)

- implementing a Bradford score system

- developing rehabilitation initiatives, and

- handling individual cases.

What is next in this Guide?

In the following chapters we provide an overview of the relevant law and provide practical advice on how to implement each element of the strategy whilst complying with that law.

Case study 1: an EEF member company that reduced its absence level from 9 % to less than 2 % in under a year

- About the case study

This case study summarises the process an actual EEF member company went through and the measures it adopted to manage more effectively both long and short-term absence with marked results over a relatively short period of time. It illustrates what can be achieved following the Steps set out in this Guide.

■ About the company

The company manufactures heavy plant vehicles and production is concentrated at two sites. There are a number of satellite sites which service the plant. The company employs just over 600 people about 50% of whom are production workers. Many are in skilled roles and their experience is very valuable. The majority of production employees are very long serving.

The company's employee relations culture had always been familial but this was put under strain when, in the late 1990s, the company was sold to a North American group and the company became financially accountable to its parent company. This led to an unprecedented redundancy exercise and morale deteriorated for a period.

■ Identifying the attendance problem

In 2002 a new Operations Director was appointed and he took a very keen interest in attendance management. Working with the HR Manager he steered a review of attendance issues, which would focus initially on production employees. Their absence level had steadily worsened over recent years reaching a high point of 9% (including both long and short-term absence) whereas the level for staff (1.5%) was considered acceptable.

The company calculated the direct and indirect costs of the absence to the business. It critically analysed the effectiveness of the existing attendance management policy and benchmarked its absence levels with similar organisations in the area.

The company had good historical attendance records and these were analysed going back three years. It produced Bradford scores (see pages 47–8) for individuals and groups of employees. This exercise showed:

- nearly 60% of the absence was accounted for by spells of absence of less than 3 days

- only 20% was due to spells of long-term absence (defined by the company as more than 3 weeks)

- colds and flu were the most common reasons given for absences

- there was a significant variation in attendance levels between the two main production sites, and

- shorter serving employees had a worse sickness record and higher Bradford scores than longer serving ones.

The benchmarking exercise also confirmed the company's view that the level of manual worker absence was excessive.

The company did have a written absence control procedure but it relied on managers using their discretion to trigger disciplinary action. Interviews with line managers who had day-to-day responsibility for discipline and attendance confirmed the HR Manager's view that they were nervous of using the existing policy and usually felt on the back foot as employees could often point to colleagues who had been treated differently.

The solution the company adopted

The company concluded that persistent short-term absenteeism was the biggest problem and should be tackled first.

It briefly considered, but then rejected on employee relations grounds, bringing back a 'waiting day' policy before company sick pay became payable which had been negotiated out two years earlier. It also considered (but rejected) introducing an attendance bonus. It felt that this would send the wrong message to employees and was unlikely to bring about change. It wanted to break down what it saw as an entrenched absence culture and needed a transparent proactive policy which could be applied uniformly.

In consultation with the recognised union for the production workers the company chose a new policy which uses a Bradford scoring system to identify employees with a frequent short-term absence problem and to trigger formal action.

Rather than specify absolute levels for triggering formal action, it is only taken against those employees whose own score in a particular month exceeds the average Bradford score for the production workforce by 10%. This makes it harder for employees to 'play the system' which can be the case if employees feel they know what a 'safe' score is.

At the same time as introducing the new scoring system the company issued revised rules for the notification of absence. These expressly stated that failure to notify or late notification might result in non-payment of company sick pay and disciplinary action. There was also an express requirement on employees on long-term absence to keep in touch with the company on a weekly basis (see below) in order to remain eligible for company sick pay.

▪ The mechanics of the policy in practice

Each month, using information from the company's computerised Time & Attendance system, the HR department produces a spreadsheet of all absences. The reasons for them are manually entered from a record produced by line managers who conduct return to work interviews.

The HR department then calculates a Bradford score for each employee and an average score for the whole shop floor. The scores take account of all absences in the last 12 months. When the policy was introduced, with effect from January 2003, the HR department had already manually inputted for each employee the previous 12 months' absence records.

Each month the HR department discusses with line managers each case where the employee's score is above the trigger level and they decide together whether they should be subject to formal action.

The company has a dedicated notice board on the shop floor which, for each month, shows the average score for the shop floor and the statistics for each team/department. The company believes this informal team competition is effective in helping break down the absence culture.

▪ How the company introduced the policy

Having involved the production workers' union representatives in developing the policy the company then paid very careful attention to informing the workforce. It held briefing sessions for the workforce and briefed line managers in advance so that they could deal with questions from their team members. It produced a short pamphlet explaining how the scoring system would work.

The workforce was given 3 months' notice of the new policy coming into effect and was made aware that absences that they had already had that calendar year would be taken into account when the new policy became operational in January 2003. However, for a transitional period of 6 months, January–June 2003, formal action was only taken in relation to those employees whose score in the month exceeded the average by 10 % and they had an instance of absence in that month. This gave employees the opportunity to improve their score by reducing their absence. The company initially intended that, after the first six months, formal action would be triggered by the score alone but it has maintained the practice of only taking action if an employee has in fact had an instance of absence in the month in question.

Formal action

Under its written policy the action the company may take follows these stages: informal counselling, a verbal then two written caution stages followed by dismissal with an appeal stage at all stages bar the informal one. Employees are told they must show an immediate lasting and substantial improvement in their attendance level. The cautions remain live on the employee's file for the same period as disciplinary warnings.

Whether the next stage is triggered obviously depends on the employee's own attendance record. However, employees are being measured against an average so if, for example, there is a flu epidemic, the average score for production employees will go up slightly. Indeed, over the winter months 2003/4, the level of absence has crept up slightly. This may be due to normal seasonal variations but it is also possible that it is slightly easier in the winter months for those employees who are determined to do so to take unnecessary time off i.e. 'play the system' because the average absence level has increased slightly anyway. There may also be a hard core of employees who, after the initial impact of the new policy, are less concerned about having formal action taken against them, at least to a certain level in the company's procedure. (NB the company's experience underlines the need to have a mechanism in the procedure to trigger action where employees' pattern of absence suggests that they are playing the system (see pages 153–4)).

Issues that came up in the early months

The employees' response

The morale of those employees with a poor attendance record and so who have been subject to formal action has inevitably been affected. As many of these were union members, the company feels that the union felt under pressure and backtracked somewhat on its initial support for the policy. However, as absence levels have generally declined, the incidence of formal action too has fallen and so the employee relations climate is settling down again.

Also, some employees found it difficult to understand that the company was not challenging the genuineness of the reason for their absence but telling them their employment was at risk because of their attendance record alone. The HR department had constantly to reinforce this message.

There has been a marked increase in employees telephoning and asking to take a day's annual leave at very short notice. This has had a knock on effect to planning as more floating holidays are being used in smaller blocks. However, subject to operational requirements, managers generally use their discretion and approve the leave. They see it as a kind of 'safety valve'.

Which absences are counted when calculating the score?

The HR department has produced guidelines for which absences should be excluded from the calculation of the score although these are not publicised to the workforce. No account is taken of absences the employee has a right to take (such as ante-natal care, time-off for dependents) and DDA-related absences are routinely excluded.

Initially, the company also excluded work-related illness or injury absences but within a very short period it was clear employees realised this was the case as there was a marked increase in entries in the Accident Book.

Absence due to work-related injuries is now counted but the company retains discretion not to take formal action if it considers it would be inequitable to do so.

◼ Slow implementation in certain departments

The HR department monitors all aspects of the new policy and it became clear very quickly that it was not being implemented rigorously in a few small areas of the business (for example, return to work interviews were missed, forms not returned to the HR department on time to help it calculate the scores, formal action was not taken, etc). The monitoring very quickly highlighted those line managers who were not comfortable with the policy or those who, for some reason, had not been fully involved in the briefing process. The company was able to take steps to deal with their concerns and fully include them.

▪ Impact on staff employees

The HR department is now more proactive in ensuring return to work interviews are conducted and that all absences are recorded for both manual and staff employees. To its surprise, the absence level for staff employees deteriorated (although not to a level considered unacceptable) and this has been attributed to better recording of their absences.

▪ Management of employees on long term sick leave

As 2003 progressed the company turned its attention to managing more proactively those employees on long-term sickness absence. The company has a generous sick pay scheme providing up to 6 months' full pay.

The company wants line managers to start staying in regular contact with employees during lengthy absences. It has retained the services of an occupational health adviser so that rehabilitation can be considered at a very early stage and to help the company obtain better quality medical reports.

However, by mid-2003 the company already had several long-term absentees and it decided that it would be too onerous for individual line managers to deal with this 'backlog'. So, as an interim measure, the HR department dealt with them without the direct involvement of the line managers.

They wrote to each individual and explained the company's new policy, set out what it would involve for them and assured the employees that they were not being singled out for detrimental treatment. Each employee was visited at home at least once and referred to the company doctor for an assessment of their functional capability. Within a few weeks all but one of these employees was back at work on a rehabilitation programme.

They are also ensuring that this supportive policy is also applied to employees who are still at work but who may have underlying chronic conditions such as arthritis or depression.

The company also considers that, with hindsight, it has been beneficial that the HR personnel were very involved in a concentrated effort to deal with existing cases. They felt they learnt a great deal very quickly about what could be done, how employees reacted, etc and they can now use this experience to better support line managers when managing their long-term absentees.

■ Impact

In under a year the company has seen its absence level fall from a peak of about 9% to less than 2%. The company is obviously delighted with the success of its initiatives; at times it was resource intensive but the investment has paid dividends.

Whilst formal action has been taken in relation to a significant number of employees, at the time of writing no employee has been dismissed due to their attendance record. Also, as attendance levels have improved so markedly, the company is reviewing the trigger levels. This is not a relaxation of the policy. Rather, because the average Bradford score for production employees is now so low, it does not take much absence for an employee to exceed it by 10%. Absent employees now stick out like a sore thumb on the monthly charts and an adjustment is necessary otherwise there is a risk employees will become resentful if the policy is applied too harshly.

The push on rehabilitating employees back to work is a very visible initiative. It has been very well received by the workforce who can see their colleagues being helped back into work in a supported and structured way. Any suspicions the workforce had about it dissipated very quickly.

The company is also considering building on its arrangements for occupational health support by bringing a practitioner on site for two days a month. The company expects this to have a further impact on reducing the incidence of long-term and short-term sickness absence.

Legal overview

Introduction

In this section of the Guide we briefly set out the legal principles which underpin many of the recommendations we make in the following sections. Following these recommendations will help employers to comply with the law as well as manage their employees' attendance.

In legal terms, the most important consideration for an employer managing individual employees who are ill or injured (whether they are working or are on sick leave) is the need to avoid liability for disability discrimination and unfair dismissal. Employees who are dismissed also have other statutory entitlements, such as the right to a written statement of reasons for dismissal and rights during notice. There may also be contractual rights. From 1 October 2004, employers will also have to comply with statutory procedural rules when taking certain types of action against their employees. These legal principles are summarised in the following pages.

Employers also owe a duty of care to employees not to cause them harm as well as having an obligation to maintain a safe system of work under health and safety legislation. Those employers who do not comply with these obligations obviously run a greater risk of higher sickness absence levels as well as the risk of successful litigation and higher insurance premiums.

Overlap between the Disability Discrimination Act and rehabilitation

● Is rehabilitation ever a legal requirement?

As will be clear from the introduction to this Guide, we believe employers who are committed to increasing rehabilitation opportunities for their employees will see, over time, an improvement in attendance levels and a reduction in dismissal/disability discrimination litigation. It may also improve their standing with employers' liability insurers. However, it would be a mistake to see rehabilitation as an entirely voluntary option.

There is no general legal requirement on an employer to consider rehabilitation for every employee who is unable to continue working because of illness or injury. However, if the employee qualifies for protection under the Disability Discrimination Act 1995 then there is a legal duty on an employer to make reasonable adjustments to working arrangements which have a detrimental impact on an employee (see pages 20–24).

There is a good deal of overlap between the issues an employer must consider under this legal duty and a voluntary rehabilitation approach.

Even if an employee's illness or injury does not meet the definition of a disability under the DDA then the employee may still claim unfair dismissal protection if he or she has at least one year's continuous employment (see pages 24–6). Unfair dismissal law indirectly imposes an obligation to consider rehabilitation-type steps because a tribunal may find unfair an ill-health dismissal if:

● there has been no meaningful consultation with the employee, including consideration of medical evidence

● the employer has not entertained simple inexpensive short-term steps (such as a phased return to work) which would have made the difference between the employee remaining absent and returning to work, and/or

● the employer has not considered alternative employment before dismissal.

Managing long-term absence against the backdrop of the DDA

There is concern that the DDA has introduced an undesirable level of uncertainty in the management of ill-health absence. There is no easy solution but we believe that if employers follow the steps in this Guide, in particular putting more emphasis on rehabilitation to get sick employees back to productive work more quickly, companies will be in a stronger position to meet their business needs and yet manage their obligations under the DDA.

Who is protected under the DDA?

In summary, an employee is protected from disability discrimination if he or she meets the definition of a disability in the Disability Discrimination Act 1995 by virtue of having a mental or physical impairment that has a substantial and long-term effect on his or her ability to carry out day-to-day activities. Normally the employee must have had the disability for at least a year or a condition that is likely to last for at least that long but this rule may be relaxed for certain progressive conditions. Once a person qualifies under the legislation, if they then recover they remain protected in relation to their 'past' disability.

Full details of the definition of a disability can be found at para 3.1.17 of the 2003/04 EEF Employment Guide (see also www.employmentguide.org.uk). The legislation does not apply to companies that employ fewer than 15 people although this exemption is to be removed from 1 October 2004.

What amounts to prohibited discrimination?

The definition of disability discrimination poses four questions:

1   Has the employer treated the disabled person in a particular way for a reason relating to the person's disability? (It is irrelevant whether the employer knew that the person was disabled, provided the reason for the treatment is in fact linked to the person's disability (see pages 18–19)).

2   If it has, was that treatment less favourable than the treatment that the employer has given, or would give, to someone to whom that reason did not apply (see pages 18–19)?

3   If it was, was the employer justified in treating the disabled person in that way? If it was not justified, then it has discriminated unlawfully (see pages 19–20).

4   Where the duty to make reasonable adjustments applies has the employer met that duty or can it justify its failure to do so (see pages 20–24)[1]?

These questions are considered in more detail overleaf.

Code of Practice

The Government has published a Code of Practice giving guidance on avoiding disability discrimination. This Code must be taken into account by employment tribunals when they are considering a disability discrimination claim, if it is relevant to the issue they are considering. Whilst the Code provides very useful guidance in some respects, its main weakness is the failure to give detailed guidance on dismissals and we are reliant on case law to fill that gap. The provisions of the Code and relevant case law are taken into account in this Guide.

The full text of the 'Code of Practice for the elimination of discrimination in the field of employment against disabled persons or persons who have had a disability' is available online: www.drc-gb.org/law/codes.asp.

What amounts to less favourable treatment?

If an employee is disabled, it is unlawful for the employer to treat him or her less favourably than it treats others for a reason linked to the individual's disability or past disability, unless it has justification for doing so (although, from 1 October 2004, it will not be possible to justify certain types of treatment (see pages 19–20).

It is important to note that the question, on whether there has been less favourable treatment, focuses on the reason for the treatment at issue, not the individual's disability. It is not difficult for an employee to establish

---

1 Note, however, that from 1 October 2004, it will no longer be possible to justify a failure to make reasonable adjustments; either an adjustment will be reasonable or it will not.

that they have been treated less favourably. Take, for example, the case of an employee who is disabled through a back injury that has resulted in a long period of sickness absence and the employee's eventual dismissal. The reason for the employee's dismissal was the sickness absence, not the back injury. The relevant question is, would the employer have dismissed an employee who had not been off sick that long; the comparison is not with another employee who has been off sick for the same length of time albeit for a different illness or injury.

■ What is the duty to make reasonable adjustments?

Before an employer can establish that it was justified in discriminating against a disabled employee (see below), it must be able to show that it has met its duty to make reasonable adjustments to accommodate the individual (see pages 20–24 for more detail). This could, for example, involve a company modifying its usual triggers for a review of attendance (see pages 157–8). A company may also need to consider alterations to job content or adaptations to equipment, or redeployment to another job, as an alternative to dismissal (see pages 21–2).

■ What is the test for justifying less favourable treatment?

It will usually be fairly simple to establish whether the disabled person has been treated less favourably. The more significant questions will, therefore, usually be the third and fourth ones set out in pages 17–18.

As to the question whether the employer was justified in treating the individual in a particular way, the test is not difficult to meet. However, from 1 October 2004, the legislation will be amended to prohibit employers from discriminating against a disabled person simply on the basis that he or she is disabled (for example, where the employer discriminates on the basis of prejudice or stereotype). From that date, such treatment cannot be justified. In practice, as is the case at the time of writing, the change will mean that the employer needs to establish that it had a reason for treating the individual in the way that it did, and that reason was relevant to the circumstances of the particular case and not merely minor or trivial. In the example of the employee with a back injury given in pages 18–19 above, therefore, the employer would need to show that the reason it dismissed the employee was because his or her absence was having an impact on the business that was more than minor or trivial. An employer may be able to justify its actions even if it did not know at the time that the employee was disabled. It is very important to note, however, that before an employer can establish justification, it must also show that it has met its duty to make reasonable adjustments (see below, pages 20–24).

In dealing with the issue of justification, the Code gives these examples:

- A significant expected deterioration in performance linked to a person's disability might justify a decision not to recruit that person.

- A belief that other employees or customers would be uncomfortable working with a disabled person would not justify a decision not to recruit that person.

- An employer would not be justified in dismissing a disabled employee for taking 'very little more' time off for sickness than other employees.

The duty to make reasonable adjustments in more depth

This section gives further advice on what is, in practice, the most important aspect of the disability discrimination legislation, that is the duty it places on employers to consider making reasonable adjustments to accommodate people with disabilities. Helping employers meet this duty is central to the advice set out in this Guide.

If an employer unjustifiably[2] fails to meet this duty, that in itself amounts to an act of disability discrimination. Furthermore, an employer cannot justify treating a person unfavourably for a reason relating to his or her disability unless it has first met its duty to consider reasonable adjustments.

---

2 Note, however, that from 1 October 2004 it will no longer be possible to justify a failure to make reasonable adjustments; either an adjustment will be reasonable or it will not.

■ To whom is the duty to make reasonable adjustments owed?

There is no length of service qualification for protection under disability discrimination legislation, unlike unfair dismissal legislation. A company may owe this duty to existing employees, whether they were disabled when they were recruited or have become disabled since they were employed. An employer may also owe the duty to a disabled person who has applied to it for a job, or has told the employer that he or she is considering applying for a job.

The duty arises, however, only where the employer's employment practices, or the physical features of its premises, put the disabled person at a disadvantage compared with non-disabled people. Furthermore, the disadvantage caused must be more than minor or trivial.

An employer is under no duty to make adjustments for an individual if it neither knows, nor could reasonably be expected to know, that the individual is disabled and is likely to be put under a disadvantage by the employer's current practices or premises. The problem, though, is that it may not always be clear until proceedings have started (or even finished) who in a company knows what about an employee's condition. For example, a tribunal might decide that a line manager and/or the personnel department knew enough to be on reasonable notice that the employee had a disability, even though the employee had never directly declared it, for example on a pre-employment medical questionnaire.

However, an employer that takes the appropriate steps set out in this Guide may meet its duty to make reasonable adjustments, even if it is not directly aware that the individual is disabled. So, an employer who has followed good rehabilitation practice is likely to be held, albeit unwittingly, to have met its duty to make reasonable adjustments.

There are special rules on how the duty to make adjustments is split between the employer of an agency worker and the company to which the worker is sent to work. These are set out in para 3.1.56 of the 2003/04 EEF Employment Guide (www.employmentguide.org.uk).

■ Does the DDA suggest what adjustments we should consider?

Yes. The legislation lists some of the potential adjustments that an employer might need to consider. They are set out in full here because of their central importance to the legislation and the overlap with the rehabilitation measures suggested in Step 5:

- adjusting premises to accommodate the disabled person, which could include adjusting fixtures, fittings, furniture, equipment, entrances and exits (although an employer will not be expected to alter any aspect of its premises that was adapted to meet the building regulations on access and facilities for disabled people)
- allocating the disabled person's duties to another person
- transferring the disabled person to another job, where there is an existing vacancy
- altering the disabled person's working hours
- assigning the disabled person to a different place of work
- allowing the disabled person time off work for rehabilitation, assessment or treatment
- giving or arranging training for the disabled person
- acquiring or modifying equipment
- modifying instructions or reference manuals
- modifying procedures for testing or assessment
- providing a reader or interpreter, and/or
- providing supervision[3].

In relation to rehabilitation, the Code points out: 'A newly disabled employee is likely to need time to readjust. For example, an employer might allow: a trial period to assess whether the employee is able to cope with the current job, or a new one; the employee initially to work from home; a gradual build-up to full-time hours… additional job coaching may be necessary to enable a disabled person to take on a new job.'

---

3 With effect from 1 October 2004 the list of potential adjustments is expanded to include 'training or mentoring for the disabled person or any other person' (which may include disability awareness training) and other forms of support in addition to supervision.

● What is a 'reasonable' adjustment?

It may not be necessary for an employer to take any of these steps. This is because the duty is to take whatever steps are reasonable in the circumstances of the particular case. Many different factors may, therefore, need to be taken into account when assessing what adjustments, if any, are reasonable.

The legislation says that these issues in particular can be taken into account when considering what adjustments would be reasonable:

● The effect that the adjustment would have on the disabled person's disadvantage. For example, it might not be reasonable to expect an employer to make an adjustment that would achieve only a small improvement in the output of someone who was significantly under-productive, especially if the adjustment would be costly or disruptive.

● The extent to which it is practicable for the company to make the adjustment. It might not, for example, be reasonable for an employer needing to fill a post urgently to have to wait for an adjustment to be made to allow a disabled person to be employed, unless a temporary adjustment or arrangement could be made until the permanent adjustment was in place.

● The cost to the employer of making the adjustment, which includes use of staff and other resources and disruption, as well as direct money costs. The Code says that it would be reasonable for an employer to spend at least as much on an adjustment to enable it to retain a disabled employee, including any retraining, as it might spend on recruiting and training a replacement.

● The size of the employer's financial and other resources.

● What financial or other assistance the company may have in making the adjustment. The disabled person him or herself is likely to be the most valuable source of advice on what adjustments would be appropriate, but advice and financial or other support may also be available from specialist agencies or the Government (see page 66).

Companies can obtain advice on the application of these factors in specific cases from their EEF Association.

● Can an employer justify failing to make an adjustment?

From 1 October 2004, employers will no longer be able to justify a failure to make a reasonable adjustment; either an adjustment will be reasonable or it will not. Until then, though, an employer can justify failing to make an adjustment but only in limited circumstances. It will not normally be able to justify treating the individual unfavourably for a reason relating to his or her disability. The only exception to this is if the employer would have been justified in treating the individual unfavourably, even if it had complied with its duty. Take, for example, an employer that fails to make a reasonable adjustment to the recruitment process for an internal vacancy to accommodate an employee unable to perform his or her original job, and then rejects that employee's application for the vacancy for a reason relating to his or her disability. The employer can justify rejecting the application if it can show that the employee would not have met the requirements for the job even if reasonable adjustments had been made.

Health and safety requirements when employing people with disabilities

It should be remembered that the Workplace (Health, Safety and Welfare) Regulations 1992 expressly require employers to equip rest rooms and rest areas with seating that is adequate for the number of disabled people they employ and suitable for them. Further, the Regulations stipulate that parts of the workplace used by disabled people must be organised in a way that takes their needs into account, particularly in relation to doors, passageways, stairs, showers, washbasins, lavatories and workstations.

Unfair dismissal

● General principles

If an employee is dismissed for sickness absence, that is, on the grounds of incapability, after being continuously employed for a year or more, the company must be able to show that it acted reasonably in treating the employee's attendance record as a sufficient reason for dismissal, if it wishes to avoid a finding of unfair dismissal. In broad terms this involves:

- consulting the employee about his or her attendance record, the reasons for it and the impact it was having on the company (see pages 104–11 and 149–53)

- explaining to the employee the possible repercussions of his or her attendance record for the employee's continued employment and giving the employee an opportunity to improve (see pages 104–11 and 149–54)

- gathering medical evidence on the employee's current condition and on when he or she would be fit to resume work (it may not be necessary for unfair dismissal purposes to obtain medical evidence in cases of intermittent, unrelated absences, but it is still advisable to do so in order to avoid liability for disability discrimination (see pages 159–60))

- considering whether there was any other work that it could offer the employee that was suitable for the employee to do, if the employee's condition made it impossible for him or her to return to his or her original job in the foreseeable future

- reasonably concluding that the impact that the employee's poor attendance was having on the business could no longer be accepted, and

- giving the employee a right of appeal (see Appendix 1).

From 1 October 2004, employers will also have to observe statutory procedural rules otherwise the dismissal will be held to be automatically unfair (see pages 27–31).

Dismissals for frequent short-term absenteeism

Slightly different considerations apply if the employee is dismissed not for long-term ill-health absence but due to frequent short-term absence.

If, despite the approaches recommended in this Guide (see Step 6: Tackling frequent short-term absence), an employee's attendance record is still unsatisfactory, the employer will consider dismissal. There comes a time when tribunals will accept that it is reasonable for an employer to say 'enough is enough'. It is for each employer to decide when that point has been reached, but it is for the tribunal to decide whether the employer has followed a fair process for any dismissal (and that includes treating employees consistently – see page 154).

Companies who take the steps recommended in this Guide normally see a significant improvement in the level of frequent short-term absence. However, for the minority of employees who do not improve, the employer may be at risk of acting in breach of the DDA if it dismisses and it turns out the employee had a qualifying disability. Also the dismissal may be unfair even if the employee has an underlying illness or injury that doesn't qualify as a disability.

It is for this reason that we advise that employers normally seek medical evidence even in cases of dismissal for intermittent absence (see pages 159–60).

● Frustration of contract

In certain rare circumstances, and this may include a catastrophic illness, an employment contract can be terminated by the operation of a legal principle known as 'frustration'. A contract is frustrated if some development occurs that means that the contract can no longer be performed, or it can only be performed in a way that is radically different from what was originally envisaged. The most common examples of when this might apply are where an employee is imprisoned for a criminal offence or becomes seriously ill.

Where the principle of frustration applies, the employee's contract is brought to an end by the operation of the principle rather than by dismissal. As a result, the employee is not entitled to claim unfair dismissal. It is difficult to predict with certainty, however, when the principle of frustration will apply as it depends on all the circumstances. If the employee's contract itself provides for the payment of sickness benefits for a certain period, the contract is unlikely to be frustrated during that period at least. Even after that, it is difficult to know how long an employee's absence would have to be before an employment tribunal would be satisfied that the fundamental basis of the contract has been destroyed. It is advisable, therefore, for a company always to follow a fair procedure in dealing with an employee who is long-term sick, rather than relying on the principle of frustration.

Pregnancy-related absence

Pregnancy-related conditions are a common cause of absence but under sex discrimination and unfair dismissal legislation pregnancy-related absence is given a protected status. If an employee is dismissed wholly or mainly because of a period of sickness absence that relates to the employee's pregnancy, then her dismissal will automatically be unfair, regardless of her length of service. This principle applies whenever the dismissal occurred, so it is unfair to dismiss a woman for a pregnancy-related sickness absence (such as post-natal depression) even if it extends long after the end of maternity leave.

It is also unlawful sex discrimination to dismiss a woman for sickness absence linked to pregnancy or absence during maternity leave or to subject her to any action short of dismissal (such as excluding her from payment of a bonus or promotion) on such grounds.

Employers should always seek the advice of their EEF Association before dismissing or taking any other action against a pregnant employee or an employee who has recently been on maternity leave.

Introduction of statutory procedural rules from 1 October 2004

■ Purpose

From 1 October 2004, employers will be required to follow statutory procedural rules when taking certain types of action against their employees. The legislation will apply to a wide variety of circumstances, including discipline and dismissal, demotion, transfer and the handling of grievances.

The rationale for the legislation is that, if employees are properly informed in advance of the employer's reasons for taking action against them, are given an opportunity to state their case and are given a right of appeal, employees are less likely to be disgruntled and so fewer employees will bring claims to employment tribunals.

At the time of writing the legislation has not been finalised but we will be issuing detailed guidance in due course. The text below is only a summary of the new rules, it should not be treated as definitive guidance. Whilst we have taken account of the new rules in setting out our recommendations in the Guide we suggest that employers seek advice on all cases where the procedural rules apply and on all dismissals.

● To what kind of employment disputes do the statutory procedural rules apply?

The legislation introduces two new mandatory procedures:

- a statutory discipline and dismissal procedure which employers will have to follow (or potentially face significant penalties (see page 30)) whenever they are contemplating dismissing an employee or taking certain forms of action short of dismissal, on the grounds of conduct or capability. Importantly, the new mandatory procedural rules will not apply to the warning or 'caution' stage of a disciplinary procedure or a procedure for managing attendance (for more on the significance of this distinction see pages 149–53). Nor will it apply to paid suspensions (for example for the purposes of investigating whether an employee who claims to be fit enough to continue working is in fact fit enough). However, the rules will apply to other kinds of action short of dismissal relevant to the management of sickness absence such as withholding sick pay, demotions, redeployment, transfers, etc.

- a statutory grievance procedure. At the time of writing the Government has said it intends for this purpose to define a grievance as 'a complaint by an employee about action which his employer has taken or is contemplating taking in relation to him' and which could form the basis of a complaint to an employment tribunal (for example a complaint about withholding sick pay).

The legislation applies to most types of employment dispute, not just cases of unfair dismissal. If an employee makes a successful complaint about certain treatment (for example, a failure to make a reasonable adjustment under the DDA) the employment tribunal can increase the award of damages it would have made anyway under that legislation by between 10 and 50 % if the employer failed to comply with its new procedural obligations in dealing with the employee's grievance.

● What do the statutory procedures require employers to do?

The new statutory procedural rules will require companies to follow a more formal procedure (involving formal letters and meetings) than many will be used to.

> In summary, the statutory discipline and dismissal procedure requires an employer to:
>
> ● before a meeting, inform the employee in writing of the reason for taking the action
>
> ● hold a meeting with an employee before taking the action
>
> ● give the employee a reasonable opportunity to respond to the employer's case
>
> ● notify the employee of the decision, and
>
> ● give the employee a right of appeal.

There are corresponding steps for the handling of a grievance.

These statutory provisions override an employer's own procedure, even a contractual one, in so far as the employer's provisions fall short of them.

There are a few very limited exceptions where the procedures will not apply. There is one in particular that may be relevant when managing cases of sickness absence. The procedure does not apply where it is not practicable to commence it or comply with its provisions within a reasonable period. This may be the case, for example, where the employee is very sick (although the employer would need to take advice on the prognosis before concluding that it did not need to follow the procedure). However, the employer's other legal obligations still remain – for example, to handle a dismissal fairly and consider the duty to make reasonable adjustments under the DDA. Until the legislation is well established companies would be wise to seek advice before relying on the exemption.

● Which employees are covered by the new procedural rules?

In theory all employees irrespective of length of service are covered. In practice, whether the employer risks a penalty and of what type depends on what complaint, if any, an employee makes to an employment tribunal, as the penalties (see this page below) for breaching the statutory rules are tied to employment tribunal claims. Unfortunately, the employer may not know in advance what claims may result.

If the employer has dismissed the employee then whether the procedure has been breached would form part of the employee's unfair dismissal complaint. As there are many types of special unfair dismissal complaints (on health and safety grounds, etc) where no length of service is required, in our view, it is safest to ensure the rules of the statutory discipline and dismissal procedure apply to all employees irrespective of service and not just those with one year's service (the qualifying period for claiming 'ordinary' unfair dismissal).

Similarly, the employee's complaint to the tribunal may allege that the employer has breached the statutory grievance procedure, for example, where the employee makes a complaint to the employment tribunal about equal pay, unlawful deductions from wages, discrimination etc. Employees do not need any length of service to bring these grievance-type claims. We suggest, therefore, that the statutory rules be applied to all employees raising an internal grievance.

● What are the penalties for the employer of not following the statutory procedural rules?

If the employer does not follow the statutory procedural rules:

- the dismissal will be automatically unfair, and

- employment tribunals can increase compensation by between 10 and 50%.

Where it is the employee who fails to comply with the statutory procedural rules (for example, fails unreasonably to attend a meeting, or fails to appeal) the tribunal has a corresponding power to reduce compensation by between 10 and 50%.

Similar penalties follow for failure to follow the statutory grievance procedure although, ultimately, the employee may be barred from pursuing a complaint to tribunal if he or she has failed to put the grievance in writing to the employer.

- Importance of keeping records of action taken prior to dismissal

Under the new procedural legislation employers will have a statutory obligation to inform employees in writing why they are contemplating taking certain action against them (including dismissal and other penalties (see page 28)). It is not yet clear how much information tribunals will expect employers to give employees. However, this requirement is an added reason for employers to keep good records of action taken to manage individual employees' attendance.

Statutory right to be accompanied

All workers have the statutory right to be accompanied by a work colleague or certified trade union official of their choice at a disciplinary, dismissal or grievance hearing, if they reasonably request to be. For these purposes, a disciplinary hearing is defined widely as a hearing that could result in the employer giving the worker a warning or taking some other action in relation to the worker. It will, therefore, cover many (but not all) of the types of meetings employers typically hold with employees to consider their attendance if it results in action being taken against them. This includes informal counselling meetings which are recorded for the purposes of establishing that the next stage in any procedure is formal action for a particular employee. In effect, the courts treat these meetings as the first stage of a formal procedure. The right will, from 1 October 2004, also apply to any meeting under the new statutory discipline and dismissal and grievance procedures (see pages 27–31).

Summary of employees' entitlements on dismissal

Despite all the measures set out in this Guide, an employer may decide that there is no alternative but to dismiss an employee. For employees dismissed because of long-term absence their dismissal will be on the grounds of incapability. For those dismissed because of their frequent short-term absence record, dismissal will usually be for 'some other substantial reason' (SOSR) (see para 4.2.33 of the 2003/04 EEF Employment Guide or www.employmentguide.org.uk). In both cases, the employer should:

- give the employee a right of appeal. From 1 October 2004 it will be mandatory to do this (see Appendix 1)

- give the employee whatever notice of dismissal he or she is entitled to under his or her contract

- ensure that the employee is paid any other benefits to which he or she is entitled, such as accrued holiday pay, and

- provide written reasons for dismissal (see also Appendix 1).

Before dismissing, however, the employer must take care not to breach any contractual rights the employee may have (see page 109) such as any rights under a permanent health insurance scheme, which can result in claims for substantial damages.

These rights are set out in more detail in Appendix 1.

Clearly define roles within the company

Introduction

Organisations differ markedly depending on their size, sector, culture, unionised status etc, but, in EEF's experience, companies have the best odds for maximising attendance, improving employees' rehabilitation prospects and establishing a strong safety culture where:

- Senior managers take primary overall responsibility for developing and ensuring implementation of a strategy for meeting these goals and the workforce is left in no doubt that this is a senior management-led initiative and a priority for action.

- Line managers, rather than the personnel function, have the key day-to-day responsibility for managing attendance issues, for example, conducting return to work interviews.

- Line managers are trained to perform their roles, which includes helping them develop an awareness of 'medical incapacity' and the business reasons for the measures set out in this Guide.

Where there is a personnel function they support senior and line managers in this programme. By monitoring they can check that line managers are adhering to guidelines and so ensure employees are treated consistently thereby reducing the risk of successful litigation. In smaller companies without a personnel function, the same controls can be assigned to a member of senior management.

What is involved in making the most of these roles is considered below.

Leading the strategy – the role of senior managers

Research, and our own experience, show that the lowest absence rates are reported in organisations where senior management has primary overall responsibility for managing attendance. For example, in its survey 'Absence and labour turnover 2003 – the lost billions'[4] the CBI showed that absence rates decline to 2.2% on average where senior managers (rather than line managers or personnel) are primarily responsible for attendance, compared to an overall average of 3%.

Why might this be? For a number of reasons:

- If senior managers take – and are seen to take – responsibility for developing and ensuring implementation of a strategy for improving attendance and improving employees' prospects for rehabilitation employees are obviously going to take note.

- Senior managers can give a clear message to the workforce that maximising attendance is a top priority and signal that everyone will be subject to the same approach. This helps line managers who are reticent about dealing with sickness absence because, for example, they feel embarrassed about asking questions and uncomfortable contacting staff at home.

- Without positive action from the top to change a company's culture, line managers will inevitably see attendance management including rehabilitation initiatives as the personnel function's job, which can result in blurred lines of responsibility and loss of focus.

- Line managers are likely to see only the information on attendance levels for their department whereas, if senior managers have responsibility, they will usually see company-wide information. By seeing the bigger picture, they are more likely to spot patterns or problem areas.

---

4 'Absence and labour turnover 2003, the lost billions: addressing the cost of absence', ISBN 0 85201 554 2, available from the CBI: www.cbi.org.uk/bookshop, Tel: 020 7395 8233.

- Senior managers may not have as many qualms as line managers about a union's reaction to a step change in tackling short-term absence problems.

Key elements of senior management's role

To be most effective in managing attendance problems and improving employees' prospects for rehabilitation senior managers need to:

- Set up a review team or working group to:
  - review how absence is recorded and measured and, if necessary, adopt new methods (see pages 45–8)
  - set priorities and targets for action, and check that risk assessments have been carried out (see pages 40–42)
  - take the lead in informing and involving the workforce of a new strategy (see pages 56–60), and
  - ensure the company has ready access to occupational health advice (see pages 61–9).

- On an ongoing basis:
  - make attendance a regular agenda item at management meetings
  - monitor attendance levels at company level in order to see the bigger picture, spot patterns or trends, or signs of inconsistency and circulate anonymised statistics to line managers and other supervisors and, where appropriate, to shop stewards or other employee representatives
  - ensure line managers carry out their operational responsibility for attendance issues and fully participate in the strategy (for example, check they are actually conducting return to work interviews and are maintaining contact with employees on long-term sick leave). The way managers handle attendance issues should be a factor in their appraisals. We suggest they should not be judged on the statistics alone as some absence is inevitable. Some companies make it a specific issue when considering performance related-pay but senior management needs to be vigilant to ensure line managers do not become overzealous in

> trying to achieve crude targets – which may result in hardship and litigation
>
> – keep under review the factors which may be revealed as underlying reasons for absence, such as the environment and physical working conditions
>
> – examine the quality of supervision, not only in terms of operational ability but also in interpersonal and communication skills. The training of line management in these skills must not be neglected, and
>
> – ensure everyone understands their obligations to keep health information confidential and observe the requirements of the Data Protection Act 1998 (see pages 48–55).

In addition to performing the above roles, senior managers must be trained to give support and guidance to line managers. This is essential to ensure that the measures are implemented in a coherent and consistent way otherwise there may be inconsistency in interpretation and of treatment in individual cases. These are significant causes of grievances and can lead to successful claims of unlawful discrimination and/or unfair dismissal.

What aspects of attendance management should line managers be responsible for?

> Line managers should:

- play a central role in a case management approach to employees on long-term absence

- be the main point of contact for an employee phoning in sick. The practicalities of this are dealt with in detail on pages 164–8.

- conduct return to work interviews, promptly and without exception, and irrespective of the duration of the absence (see pages 168–78). This means they must be given the time to deal with attendance issues, otherwise immediate operational issues will inevitably take priority

- keep their own attendance records

- be regularly briefed on patterns and about progress in achieving targets across the company. They should be given sufficient information about attendance levels in other departments to be able to make comparisons with their own. This helps line managers to review their own performance (but see also page 184 on team competition)

- make attendance statistics a regular subject of team or departmental meetings, and

- be encouraged (if not required) to give their views on crucial issues such as working arrangements, job design, etc and other factors which might be influencing attendance figures. Ideally, line managers should have some control over these issues but, if they do not, there must be a mechanism for feeding back their views to those who do.

Personnel support

The personnel or HR function, whatever its size, plays a key role in an action plan for managing attendance but, in EEF's experience, the most effective plans do not give the personnel function the responsibility for delivery. Instead, it acts as a specialist cell, providing the procedural machinery, the written guidelines, the records, and the induction scheme. Crucially, it should also ensure that the company's guidelines are observed. So, the personnel function:

- monitors information on which employees have been absent and why. It monitors whether line managers are conducting return to work interviews, are making and maintaining contact with employees covered by medical certificates and are taking any other steps the company has adopted and at the appropriate time

- ensures that line managers are trained in the consistent application of established procedures: inconsistencies cause employee relations difficulties and can turn an otherwise fair dismissal into an unfair one

- provides the necessary training, advice and support to line management conducting home visits, return to work interviews etc

– but it does not conduct those interviews itself (see also pages 83–4 for some practical issues relating to home visits)

- ensures line managers have the necessary personal and managerial skills. This includes some training in the skills of employee counselling on those matters which the company has the power to influence

- participates in the more advanced stages of a procedure for dealing with attendance problems

- should provide easy to complete forms for recording absence and details of any discussions held

- should be the main point of contact for occupational health support and, in conjunction with line managers, writes the letters seeking medical information (see pages 93–8)

The personnel function should also ensure that line managers:

- stick to any guidelines for considering rehabilitation and understand that these measures potentially apply to employees who are not yet taking long-term sickness absence

- understand the impact of their own behaviour on their subordinates and so are encouraged to constantly examine their own performance and attitude on such issues as allocation of work and equal and fair treatment of employees, and

- make a contribution to improving the working environment, physical conditions and job design. ACAS has produced guidance which gives more detail on the organisational issues, such as job design, and their influence on attendance. Called 'Absence and Labour Turnover' it is available online at www.acas.org.uk/publications/b04.html

Companies without a formal personnel function

Those member companies without an in-house personnel function can meet the objectives set out in this Guide by:

- Seeking the assistance of their EEF Association to identify which aspects of the personnel role identified above can, in any event, be undertaken by a member of the senior management team instead. EEF can provide training for that person.

- For any remaining aspects (such as producing standard forms for line managers to use), EEF can provide these services, too.

- Seeking the advice of their EEF Association on individual cases and on general issues such as accessing suitable occupational health advice.

Health and safety representatives

Statutory employee health and safety representatives have a vital role to play in maintaining a safe system of work. Carrying out risk assessments, encouraging a safety culture and ensuring compliance generally with health and safety legislation are also essential ingredients in a successful strategy for eliminating unnecessary absence. These representatives should, therefore, be consulted on any initiatives for reducing absenteeism and improving the prospects of employees being successfully rehabilitated back into work.

Identify priorities for action

What are the key questions a company needs to answer?

In order to manage attendance more effectively companies have to be able to answer the following questions:

- How much does sickness absence cost the company?

- Is there a higher incidence of work-related injuries in particular areas? Are there any physical or process- related hazards, which are making employees sick (including mental health disorders)?

- Are sickness absences mainly long-term or short-term?

- Are they mainly covered by medical certificates or are there a large number of odd self-certificated days off? Are there any patterns, perhaps clustered around public or school holidays?

- Is the problem a general one affecting the entire workforce, or do only a few employees or certain areas of the business have substantial levels of absence? Are certain teams worse than others? Why might that be?

- Has management tolerance of slack attendance created a culture in which frequent absence is the norm? Are there any discernible causes for the absences that are within the company's power to control, such as working conditions or management style?

- In which areas of the business is absenteeism most disruptive?

- Who decides if and when an employee is fit to return to work?

Armed with answers to these questions management can start to identify priorities for action, which may differ from department to department.

How to answer these questions

In order to answer these questions, a company needs to:

- diligently carry out health and safety risk assessments (see page 42)

- have a reliable system, which managers are trained in to ensure consistency, for recording and monitoring who has been absent and why, and for how long, and

- put in place mechanisms so that occupational health support, particularly external advisers, can feed back to the company any observations that might suggest that the company can control some of the reasons for employees' absence.

Each of these issues is dealt with below.

Calculating the cost of absence

The CBI in its 2002/3 survey of absence and labour turnover (see pages 34–5) found that in 2002, 6.8 days were lost on average per employee which, it says, is the equivalent of 2.9% of total working time. For manual workers, this average rises to 8.4 days or 3.7% of total working time[5]. Projecting these figures across the UK workforce, the CBI estimates that over 166 million working days were lost in 2002 due to absence at a direct cost of more than £11bn.

Why calculate the cost?

Many employers do not quantify the cost of their absence levels. Fewer share those figures with the workforce even though doing so can have a sobering effect on employees and their representatives. Being transparent with this information is a vital part of encouraging a high attendance culture.

---

5 These figures include absences from work for all reasons but exclude public holidays, annual leave, jury service and statutory leave such as maternity and paternity leave.

Apportioning the cost across departments also helps managers to be sure that they are targeting action on those areas of the business which are in fact contributing most to the costs. The facts may not accord with managers' subjective assessment.

In calculating the true cost of absence, companies need to count not just the direct costs (SSP and occupational sick pay, employer's NI contributions, employer's contributions to pension plus overtime or agency costs to cover the absentee) but also the indirect costs. These include the time of line managers and personnel officers, training time, the cost of providing employee assistance or occupational health services, etc and the impact on staffing levels, lost production and the impact on service delivery. Normally the indirect costs are at least equal to the direct costs.

● Risk assessments

Companies should, in accordance, with their obligations under health and safety legislation be diligently conducting risk assessments of all physical and process-related hazards including work-related stress hazards.

Effective risk assessments should eliminate some of the reasons for absence that are in the employer's control, reducing exposure to expensive litigation and help the employer meet the demands of employers' liability insurers.

A standard risk assessment approach involves identifying the main hazards, identifying who could be harmed and how, and then deciding on the steps to eliminate or control the level of risk presented by each hazard. As there is not space in this publication for detailed guidance on how to carry out a risk assessment, member companies are referred to the HSE's 'Code of Practice and Guidance on the Management of Health and Safety at Work Regulations 1999' and the free HSE leaflet 'Five Steps to Risk Assessment'[6]. EEF will also be issuing in 2004 guidance on risk assessment as part of its OHSAS 18001 management systems package. Further details are available from EEF Associations.

---

6 Available from www.hse.gov.uk, Tel: 01787 881165.

Monitoring absence

▪ Why monitor absence?

To maximise attendance, employers need to:

- collect information, and

- analyse it to enable them to identify patterns of absence for both individuals and groups of employees. We consider some of the most common tools for doing so on pages 45–8.

Armed with this information managers can identify priorities for improving the management of attendance.

Accurate attendance records will also significantly enhance the company's ability to defend any allegation of unfair dismissal or disability discrimination. Managers who base their decisions for taking action against individuals (including dismissals) on objective records rather than perceived absence levels are better placed to meet allegations of unfair or inconsistent treatment.

In addition, monitoring allows a business to see how they are doing in comparison with others. For example, how does the attendance level of the organisation's non-manual work-force compare with the national average for non-manual workers of 5.5 working days of absence per annum (equivalent to 2.4%) or that of its manual workers compare with the national average for manual workers of 8.4 working days lost (3.7%) per annum[7]?

▪ Distinction between monitoring 'absence' and 'health' information

There is a distinction between 'absence' information (for example, the fact that an employee has had one spell of absence lasting 5 days) and 'health' information (for example it was due to the flu).

It is accepted wisdom if not general practice that companies should be collecting and analysing information about which employees are absent and for how long. Employers can, however, go a step further and analyse the health reason for the absence.

---

7 CBI Survey 2002/03, see footnote 4 on page 34.

Most employers already collect, store and analyse 'health' information about their employees because generally they keep self-certificates and medical certificates. They may also keep line managers' notes and notes made by the personnel department. Below (in pages 48–55) we consider the benefits of analysing health information for a group of employees. We also briefly explain important data protection and confidentiality obligations, which can usually be satisfied if certain rules are followed.

Recording absence information

Employers should establish a simple format, applicable to all employees, for collecting information and train managers in completing it to ensure consistency. It is vital that managers stick to a uniform method of recording absence to ensure the results are more reliable and make the administrative aspects of analysing the data easier.

Who should make the records?

Whilst attendance records can be made by the personnel function, it is preferable to make it an integral part of the responsibilities of managers and supervisors, since it is they who should be responsible for managing attendance on a day-to-day basis (see pages 36–7). If they are recording data, they are more likely to spot patterns within their own departments.

Fair and lawful processing of absence information

Absence information which is held (or is intended to be held) electronically or in structured files is personal data and must be processed fairly and lawfully under the Data Protection Act 1998 (the 'DPA'). This means that:

- absence records should be stored separately to health information (see above, pages 43–4, for more on the distinction between them). An employer's obligations in relation to health information are onerous (see pages 48–55) and separate storage will help prevent a breach of the DPA

- employers must inform employees what information it is holding about them, what it is using it for (e.g. for normal employment purposes, including monitoring absence levels and administering sick pay) and who it will disclose it to. This could be done at induction, but should also be included on self-certification forms and included in a written policy or company handbook dealing with attendance

- absence records which identify individuals should only be made available to those who genuinely need to see them. Wherever possible, they should be anonymised. For example, reviewing attendance levels across a department can be done on a 'no names' basis (see also page 184 on team competition and league tables), and

- absence records should be stored securely (see page 54).

Analysing attendance records

● Introduction

In this section, we look at the analysis of attendance as opposed to health information (see pages 43–4 for more on the distinction). There are a variety of management tools for analysing attendance information but this Guide is only concerned with the most commonly used ones.

The results should be circulated for careful consideration at least quarterly to senior managers and on a monthly basis to line managers and, where appropriate, to shop stewards or other employee representatives.

It should not normally be necessary for the data being circulated to identify the individuals or the health reason for their absences (see pages 52–3 and 184).

● Main management tools and their purpose

The main management tools for analysing attendance information are the severity rate, frequency rate and analysis of the duration of spells of absence. In addition, many employers use an indicator known as the Bradford score, which helps employers to identify those employees with a high level of frequent short-term absence.

We briefly consider these indicators below (pages 46–8) and, in Appendix 2, illustrate with some hypothetical information what issues can arise.

Armed with the information generated with the help of these tools, figures for the cost of absence (see page 41) and the results of risk assessments, etc the company is better placed to:

- target its resources on the most problematic departments, and

- be clearer about the kind of action necessary – be it health and safety issues, tighter management control of short-term absence, a push for rehabilitation, consideration of adjustments under the DDA for long-term absentees, improved management training, etc.

Severity

The severity rate highlights the average number of days lost per person. It is calculated as the number of days of absence in a period divided by the average number of employees employed in that period. Another way of defining severity is by looking at the lost time percentage, which is usually the total time lost divided by the total potential working time (excluding overtime) of the workforce, expressed as a percentage.

Frequency

The frequency rate highlights the number of 'spells' of absence. There are two approaches:

a) the 'spell frequency rate' is the number of new spells of absence in a period divided by the number of employees in a particular period, or

b) the 'person frequency rate' which is the number of employees having one or more spells in a period divided by the average number of employees employed in a particular period.

Analysing the length of absence

The duration of absences can be looked at in two ways:

(a) first, by calculating the average length of a spell of absence. This is the total number of days of absence in a period divided by the number of spells of absence in that period.

(b) alternatively, by finding the median duration of the spells[8]. The
     advantage of using the median duration is that the statistics are
     not skewed by the effect of a few individuals with very long spells of
     absence.

● The Bradford score

To help them tackle frequent short-term absence many EEF member
companies are adopting the 'Bradford' scoring system. It is not clear from
where the name originates.

This relatively simple tool highlights those employees with unacceptable
levels of frequent short-term absence and is best explained by example. For
a defined period (say, 3 months) each employee is given a score calculated
as follows:

> S [spells of absence] x S [spells of absence] x D [total number of days
> of absence in that period]

Thus someone who has five spells of absence which last one day each
(5x5x5 = 125) will have a higher Bradford score than an individual who has
one episode of absence which lasts five days (1x1x5 =5).

Using the Bradford score the attendance records of individuals can then
be measured against a defined trigger level (passing which would trigger
action to manage the employee's attendance (see pages 153–6)).

However, the Bradford score can also be used to compare the attendance
levels of groups of employees, for example by age, job category, or geograph-
ical location. Managers can then use the scores to identify priority groups for
further initiatives. For example, a company with several sites may discover
that one site in particular has a high Bradford score. This might suggest that
the site be targeted for further initiatives such as revising risk assessments,
occupational health screening, management training, etc or a combina-
tion of these. These can go hand-in-hand with the rehabilitation measures
suggested in Step 5 (see pages 86–90) for managing employees on long-
term absence or those who are still working but have an illness or injury.

---

8 That is, the middle value in a distribution of duration of spells when they are ranked in
order of duration.

Without a doubt many EEF member companies have had significant success in raising attendance levels with an attendance management procedure based on the Bradford score. It works best when combined with rigorously enforced notification procedures and return to work interviews. The case study on page 7 shows how one particular EEF member company used the tool successfully to review attendance patterns to help it identify priorities for action and then used it on an ongoing basis to help it manage attendance. Whilst the formula appears to be relatively simple, companies who have success with it are those who, like the company in the case study, ensure it is transparent and take care to explain it to their employees.

Monitoring employees' health

■ Why do it?

Whilst analysing non-health data is very easy to do, analysing clinical sickness absence data requires more effort and the input of an occupational health adviser to help the company interpret the findings. There are also important obligations controlling the handling of health information (see page 50). However, in our view it is worthwhile as it helps the company prioritise interventions, particularly occupational health involvement and risk assessments. Another benefit of recording the causes of absence is that the company can compare its statistics with those for the general population or benchmark with similar organisations.

■ How to do it

An organisation that has a computerised method of monitoring sickness absence could, relatively easily, add the reason for the absence when the data is being entered.

There are two objectives:

■ first, to code the reasons for absence into groups (so, for example, it is possible to identify departments that have a particular problem with stress-related conditions), and

- second, to tag the information on the self-certificate or medical certificate for specific conditions, such as RSI.

This would require one code field and one free text field. In both cases, employers can use this information to prioritise or target interventions (such as revisiting risk assessments), introducing health screening and stress awareness training, considering investment in a physiotherapy service, etc.

We suggest that companies with workforces below 100 would not generate sufficiently reliable statistics to warrant coding the reasons for absence into groups although even for small organisations it is important to record the health information in order to analyse the actual reason given for the absence.

How to group the illnesses requires specialist advice. Nevertheless, a few groupings are consistently useful and EEF recommends the following categories:

- acute respiratory infections (e.g. sore throats and colds, bronchitis and chest infections, viral illnesses)

- back problems (e.g. sciatica, back pain, backache, lumbago, slipped disc, and prolapsed disc)

- other musculoskeletal disorders excluding back problems (e.g. neck pain, frozen shoulder, RSI, arthritis, cervical spondylosis)

- stress, anxiety and depression (including nervous debility, neurasthenia, bereavement)

- injuries (i.e. sprained ankle, fractures of bones)

- operations and medical investigations (e.g. hernia repair, cholecystectomy, hysterectomy)

- headaches and migraine, and

- all other causes.

The coding should also indicate whether the cause is considered (or alleged to be) work-related.

Handling health information

Whilst it is generally accepted that employers have a legitimate interest in collecting and analysing health information for business purposes, employees have a number of rights over, and others owe them certain duties in relation to, their own health information. They are:

- a health professional's duty of medical confidentiality (see below, pages 50–51)

- the employee's right to control access to their health information (hence the need for consent (see pages 51–2))

- the employer's obligations to treat health information fairly and lawfully under the Data Protection Act 1998 (see pages 52–4)

- the employer's implied duty of trust and confidence to their employees (see page 54) and

- employees' right to privacy under the Human Rights Act 1998 (see pages 54–5).

These rights and obligations have a significant impact on the employer's approach to collecting and analysing information about their employees' health as is explained below on pages 50–55.

Occupational health professionals' duty of medical confidentiality

Occupational health professionals (e.g. doctors or nurses who are employed by the company or independent company doctors/nurses etc) are likely to hold health information from different sources, for example:

- health questionnaires completed by an employee

- employees' self-certification forms and medical certificates

- reports from an employee's own doctor, or

- their own reports of examination of individuals.

They may use the information held to:

- treat an individual

- assess an employee's ability to perform particular duties

- consider adjustments to duties and rehabilitation, or

- monitor workforce absence for trends or patterns of ill-health.

Occupational health professionals have the same duties as employers to treat health and absence information (see pages 43–4 for more on the distinction between them) fairly and lawfully under the DPA (see pages 44–5).

They also have additional duties. The fact that a health professional is employed by or appointed by an employer does not alter the doctor/patient relationship. The BMA advises that the employer may only be given information relating to health records or details of medical examinations with the patient's informed consent[9].

However, provided he or she complies with the DPA, the occupational health professional does not need consent to provide absence (as opposed to health) information (see pages 43–4) or to interpret his or her findings for the employer. This means that, for example, the health professional does not strictly need consent to give the employer a report assessing the fitness for work of an employee who has a back problem or his or her assessment of what adjustments the employer might consider. It is, though, an ethical requirement for the occupational health professional to inform the employee of any information passed to the employer. The employer should, however, consult the employee on the information anyway (see pages 100–101 and 107–108).

● Employees' rights to control access to their health information

If an employer wants to obtain medical information from any doctor who is, or has been responsible for the clinical care of the employee, such as a GP or consultant, it must meet the detailed requirements of the Access to Medical Reports Act 1988 ('AMRA'). AMRA requires employers and doctors to follow certain procedures and a timetable when obtaining and disclosing medical information about an individual. Most importantly it requires the employer to obtain the express consent of the employee before applying for a report and it gives the employee an opportunity to see it first and request that

---

9 The Occupational Physician available on www.bma.org.uk.

changes are made to it. These rules are set out in detail in paras 3.2.69–3.2.76 of the 2003/04 EEF Employment Guide (www.employmentguide.org.uk).

Generally speaking, the strict procedural rules in the AMRA legislation do not apply to occupational health professionals and independent company doctors who are not treating or have not in the past treated the employee in the context of a doctor/patient relationship. However, the occupational health professional must still have the employee's consent to disclose 'health' information to the employer as opposed to information about absence or fitness for work (see pages 50–51).

If an employee refuses consent or withdraws consent to the health professional providing health information to the employer, the employer will not be able to see it. The occupational health professional should inform the employer that consent has been refused. It will then be for the employer to explain to the employee that it will have to make employment decisions in the absence of the full medical picture (see pages 93–4).

Even where consent has been refused, the occupational heath professional does, though, have an overriding duty of care to the employee to inform his or her employer if there are fitness for work issues which mean that the employee's health and safety would be at risk. This can be done without disclosing the underlying medical reason for the concern.

● Fair and lawful processing of health information under the Data Protection Act

General obligations

Health records which are held (or intended to be held) electronically or in structured files are personal data and must be processed fairly and lawfully under the DPA. Employees should be informed at the beginning of their employment what information about absences and health will be collected and held, what it will be used for and who it will be disclosed to.

Processing health information is intrusive. It will generally only be lawful for an employer to collect, hold, use or disclose (together, 'processing') health information if:

- it is necessary to meet legal obligations, such as to comply with health and safety obligations or not to discriminate against workers on the basis of a disability

- it is in connection with legal proceedings or

- the worker has given express consent. This means that the worker must be told clearly what information is involved and the use that will be made of it. Employers should obtain the worker's signature. Consent must be freely given. A worker must be able to say 'no' without penalty (e.g. removal of job offer, dismissal etc) and be able to withdraw consent at a later date. It will not be enough to gain a general consent at the start of employment. Employers should seek express written consent each time that new health information is gathered.

The collection and use of the health information must be a proportionate response to the particular problem. The Information Commissioner states that managers should not have access to more information about a worker's health than is necessary to carry out their management responsibilities and that in most cases this will be limited to that concerning a worker's fitness for work.

However, in companies which follow the approach to managing attendance advocated in this Guide, managers may well process quite a lot of information about individual's health, for example in back to work interviews. If companies decide to manage attendance issues in this way it is incumbent on them to also train their managers in their obligations under the DPA and their duty to keep confidential employees' health information. We have taken account of these obligations in drafting our recommendations.

There will be some cases where companies can use less intrusive information. For example, we advocate that absence reports are circulated between departments (see pages 35–6). These do not need to contain health information and should be done on an anonymous basis. Where health information is being analysed for groups of employees again the information can be anonymised and for many purposes, the health reason for the absence does not need to be identified.

Storing health information

Particular care should be taken to store health information securely. The Information Commissioner recommends that it is kept in a sealed envelope separate from other personnel information or subject to additional access controls on an electronic system.

Can an employee see what health information we hold about them?

Yes, an employee can make a subject access request to see information held about them by the employer which is either stored on computerised files or in structured paper records (see para 8.3.20 of the 2003/04 EEF Employment Guide or www.employmentguide.org.uk). It is possible for an employer to withhold some information in limited circumstances.

▪ The employer's implied duty of trust and confidence

In addition to the obligations imposed on employers by the DPA, misuse of absence or health information by the employer could in some circumstances amount to a breach of trust and confidence, entitling an employee to resign and claim constructive dismissal.

▪ The employee's right to privacy under the Human Rights Act – does it prevent employers from conducting surveillance of employees who are off sick?

There may be occasions when an employer does not believe that an employee is genuinely off sick and wishes to monitor the employee's activities covertly to establish if this is the case. This could involve someone from the company or a private investigator collecting information about a person's activities, for example by videoing them doing an activity inconsistent with their claim to be sick. However, in order to comply with the DPA, the Human Rights Act 1998 and to avoid breaching the implied term of trust and confidence, covert monitoring should only be used as a last resort and in the following circumstances:

- when it is necessary for the prevention or detection of criminal activity or equivalent malpractice. In our view, falsely claiming to be unfit for work could in some circumstances justify covert monitoring

- such monitoring should not take place in areas an individual might genuinely and reasonably expect to be private, such as inside their own house or garden

- if a private investigator is used, the private investigator must agree by contract to comply with the employer's obligations under the DPA

- the benefits to the employer must justify the significant intrusion into the individual's privacy, and

- senior management should authorise it.

These factors are also relevant where managers undertake 'spot checks' of sick employees at home (see page 178).

If the evidence indicates that an employee has been dishonest, then the employer should investigate fully. It is possible that the employee has a good explanation. If appropriate, the employer should take action under its disciplinary procedure.

Involve and inform the workforce

Introduction

If a company resolves to have a major push to maximise attendance including putting more emphasis on rehabilitation it needs to involve and inform its workforce. This gives the strategy the best odds for working and helps the company comply with its legal obligations. It will also help ensure that employees know the standards of attendance expected of them and the consequences of falling short of them. Companies should, therefore:

- consult trade unions and/or employee representatives (such as a works council or employee forum) on any new initiatives

- explain the company's approach to handling cases of long-term sickness absence

- clarify or revise an existing notification procedure. If this involves a change to employees' existing contracts of employment, then employers will have to seek agreement to the variation in the usual way or risk breach of contract/constructive dismissal and/or claims for unlawful deductions from wages (see Chapter 5.1, 'Changing contracts of employment' in the 2003/04 EEF Employment Guide, www.employmentguide.org.uk)

- ensure senior management should take the lead in briefing sessions to employees on the new strategy so that they, too, can understand why the company is taking the action it is

- follow briefing meetings with individual letters – this is especially important if there are changes to existing procedures, and

- revamp induction courses to put more emphasis on the message of 'maximum attendance' rather than just describing the absence notification procedure.

First, though, before a company rolls out information on any new initiatives to employees, it should first ensure that all line managers fully understand (and, preferably, actively support) them. They need to be prepared to answer questions from employees. The case study on page 7 shows some of the issues which can arise.

Informing employees already on long-term sickness absence of any new initiatives

Ensure that employees who are already on long-term sickness absence when an employer adopts new initiatives for managing sickness and rehabilitation are kept informed of developments. This will make the line manager's task easier when, for example, the company contacts the employee to consider rehabilitation (see pages 80–81). The company should also ensure employees who are away for other reasons (such as on maternity or parental leave) are kept informed.

Induction

The message that the company takes attendance seriously and actively manages attendance, including long-term absence, should be given a high priority in induction courses. This is especially the case if the company's analysis of attendance information suggests that, as is often true (see, for example, the case study on page 7), new starters have a worse record than longer established employees do.

Course content should cover:

- individuals' responsibility to honour: – any specific terms of their contracts, such as a notification procedure and certification rules, and

- the unwritten terms of their contracts, such as to act in good faith and in an honourable and trustworthy way

- the cost to the company of absence and its impact on service delivery. For example, include information on the cost to the company in the previous year and examples of the impact on performance

- how the company deals with long-term absence, including explaining the reasons behind maintaining contact throughout, the steps that might be taken to explore rehabilitation, etc

- the sickness absence reporting procedure (do not just hand out a copy of the written rules) and the qualifying conditions for sick pay entitlement

- the purpose of return to work interviews (see pages 168–78), and

- the message that, if it isn't sickness, employees shouldn't call in sick. Explain that there are statutory rights for dealing with domestic emergencies and rights to seek flexible working for those employees with children under the age of six or with children with a disability under 18. If the company has more beneficial contractual rights, such as compassionate leave, explain them. Make sure employees know the difference and how to claim those benefits and that wrongly claiming sick pay will lead to disciplinary action which may include dismissal on grounds of gross misconduct.

Remember, though, that the session should reinforce and link in with the sessions on health and safety (role of risk assessments, mutual responsibility for maintaining health and safety standards, obligations to wear protective clothing), etc.

The benefits of such an induction programme will, though, be lost if, as soon as the employee gets into the workplace, they hear a different message from colleagues (for example, in relation to absence notification rules, 'don't worry, it's never enforced') and line managers do not, by their actions or comments, reinforce the company's message.

Legal obligation to inform employees in writing of rules and procedures dealing with attendance

Although there is no legal requirement for a contract of employment to be in writing, the law does require an employer to give its employees written information on their main terms and conditions of employment, and to update this information if the details change. This information is often referred to as a 'statement of employment particulars' or a 'written statement of main terms and conditions of employment'. Full details of the information the employer must give is set out in Chapter 1.2.4 of the 2003/04 EEF Employment Guide, www.employmentguide.org.uk.

The employer must provide information on any terms and conditions relating to incapacity for work due to sickness or injury, including details of any sick pay scheme that the company operates. If there are no relevant details to give, then the information should make that clear. So, if the employer does not provide company sick pay, the information should say so.

Employers should also spell out which terms, if any, are not contractual, such as an attendance management or disciplinary procedure. We advise that these do not form part of the contract.

A written attendance management policy

A company is more likely to maximise attendance effectively if it has a clear written policy containing the rules and procedure for dealing with absence of whatever type, which is communicated to employees and which it applies consistently. For example, employees should be clearly informed of what procedure they should follow if they want to take holiday or apply for compassionate leave, and what requirements on notification and medical evidence they must meet in order to qualify for sick leave or pay.

A policy can take the form of guidance for management, or a standard document issued to all employees, or both although it is preferable that managers receive separate guidance. A checklist of the main features a policy should contain, (particularly if a company wishes to focus more on rehabilitation) is set out on pages 132–4.

Informing individual employees of the policy and making changes to it

To be effective:

- Each employee should be given a copy and asked to sign against a list of names to acknowledge receipt; don't just pin it on the notice board or send it round by e-mail.

- A copy should be given to each employee when a new policy is introduced and to all new starters on their induction.

- Where the policy is changed, ensure all employees are, at the least, given a statement of the changes. It is preferable if they are given a copy of the revised procedure itself. Obtain their signatures, acknowledging receipt.

The policy may be contractual but the employer may have expressly reserved the right to make amendments from time to time. In this case, give reasonable notice of the variation and, again, obtain employees' signatures acknowledging that they have received notification of the change. There may also be a requirement under the policy to consult employees first.

If the policy is contractual but the employer has not reserved the right to make amendments then seek agreement to any variation in the usual way (see Chapter 5.1, 'Changing contracts of employment' in the 2003/04 EEF Employment Guide, www.employmentguide.org.uk). Member companies should contact their EEF Associations for further advice.

We advise that any policy expressly states that it does not form part of the employees' contracts of employment.

Step 4

Establish ready access to occupational health support

How can we benefit from improved access to occupational health support?

Occupational health advisers are concerned both with how an employee's health can affect his or her ability to do the job and with how work and the work environment can affect an employee's health.

Employers who use occupational health services routinely are more likely to meet their obligations to make reasonable adjustments under the DDA, or to act fairly and reasonably in deciding to dismiss an individual for ill-health, particularly if they involve their occupational health advisers early, ask them the right questions and give them the right information. They can also help the employer reduce the risk of personal injury claims and, through successful rehabilitations, reduce the drain on pension schemes caused by ill-health early retirements.

A successful strategy for improving employees' prospects for rehabilitation depends upon improved access to occupational health advice although what level of support is appropriate depends on each company's own circumstances. Remember also that occupational health advisers are a key source of advice for managers but they are not a substitute for managers making their own decisions.

How can occupational health advisers support us?

We summarise below the main ways in which occupational health advisers can support managers in reducing absence due to illness.

● Reducing general risks to health within the workplace

Occupational health professionals can:

- in conjunction with health and safety advisers, advise companies on how to comply with their statutory health and safety obligations

- carry out or assist in risk assessments

- organise health promotion events, such as back care workshops (see page 186) and stress management programmes both for employees themselves and to train managers on how to spot and reduce workplace illness and stress

- manage access to and delivery of first aid services and/or running open clinics for employees

- attend health and safety committees and other relevant groups which consider the health of employees, and

- monitor the reasons for absence amongst the workforce and identify any particular problem areas (see pages 43–5), their causes and suggest remedial action.

● Reducing absence in relation to particular individuals

In relation to individuals, occupational health advisers can have a significant impact on cutting down unnecessary absence as follows:

Pre-employment screening

- First, they can assess whether individuals who are likely to be offered a job are fit enough to do it and can consider what, if any, adjustments might be possible if they have a qualifying disability under the DDA.

- They can also help a company assess a prospective employee's sickness absence record with a former employer. It is generally accepted by occupational health professionals that an employee's absence pattern over the previous two years is an indicator of the possible pattern over the next two, particularly for short-term absences and for some chronic conditions. However, employers and their occupational health adviser must take into account the obligations under the DDA not to discriminate unlawfully against employees if the absence is related to a disability (see pages 16–20).

Management of long-term sickness absence

Occupational health advisers are particularly important in the management of long-term sickness absence. They are essential to the case management approach advocated in Step 5 (see pages 75–80), which focuses on the rehabilitation of employees who would otherwise be on long-term sick leave. This approach involves a proactive and co-ordinated team effort, with input from a very early stage by the manager, the personnel function if there is one, the occupational health adviser and the employee. Continuity of advice can be helpful.

A few examples of how an occupational health adviser can be involved in a case management approach are:

- advising a manager who has just received a medical certificate suggesting the employee might have a lengthy absence (or after a succession of short medical certificates) on the possible prognosis and what might be feasible for a return to work (see pages 82–3)

- examining an employee to assess the nature of the illness, the prognosis, whether rehabilitation is an option and the form it should take

- monitoring an employee who has returned to work on a rehabilitation programme (see pages 102–103)

- advising an employee on their condition and to see if any (additional/different) medical treatment perhaps from a specialist might be beneficial

- to assess whether it would be beneficial for the company to pay for certain treatment, for example, for physiotherapy where there is a long NHS waiting list (see pages 90–93)

- to provide a second opinion on a GP's report and, where there is a conflict in the medical advice, to liaise with the GP to resolve any differences (see pages 99–100), and

- to assess employees' eligibility for long term disability benefits or retirement on health grounds.

Management of frequent short-term absence

Occupational health advisers also have a role in reducing frequent short-term absence. For example, it may become apparent in a return to work interview or in the course of a stage of the attendance management procedure that absences may be related to an underlying condition. In such cases, the employee should be referred to the occupational health adviser for an examination, triggering some or all of the actions described above.

Deciding on a level of occupational health support

The strategy set out in this Guide cannot be fully implemented without some access to occupational health support. However, the type of support that is appropriate and affordable will vary depending on the nature, size, location and range of hazards of particular companies. Some larger companies may already have their own occupational health department, consisting of either employed occupational health physicians and/or nurses; others might have a contract with independent providers of occupational health advice.

However, many companies have no access to occupational health support. These companies may well believe that the cost of a more established arrangement for occupational health support would be unjustifiable. However, when considering the cost, companies should bear in mind the significant improvements in absence levels and staff retention that implementing the strategy proposed in the Guide can bring.

Wherever possible, we recommend that companies plan ahead for accessing occupational health support as this cuts down the amount of time wasted unnecessarily searching for support when the need arises. Some companies find that establishing permanent or standing arrangements with an adviser meets their needs; for others (for example, smaller companies) an ad hoc approach will be sufficient.

The most effective advisers are those who are familiar with the way the business operates, including its approach to sickness absence, and who have a good knowledge of its site/plants and of any particular hazards.

We suggest companies consider which of the following types of support meet their needs:

- an initial audit and inspection of the site/plant, its working practices, relevant policies and procedures and its absence and health monitoring procedures

- that a designated person can telephone for advice, for example when the company receives a medical certificate which indicates a lengthy sickness absence

- conduct of medical examinations, including risk-based and general health-based assessments, assessments for job applicants and where a manager refers an employee because a potential or actual health problem has been identified

- active involvement at each stage of the case management of long-term sickness absence and rehabilitation, which may involve examining the employee, considering what measures are necessary to enable rehabilitation, liaising with GPs or other doctors, and

- reviewing employees who have recurrent short-term absences (see pages 159–60).

The company needs to be satisfied that the provider is willing to be proactively involved in case management, which can be a fluid process. Assistance may be needed at short notice, with duties ranging from medical examination, attending meetings, advising by telephone, liaising with the employee's GP etc.

Where do we obtain good quality occupational health support?

Unfortunately there is no national network in the UK of occupational health services and private provision is fragmented and of varying quality. EEF is, however, considering a number of options for improving occupational health support for its member companies. For further information, member companies should contact their EEF Associations. There is also a list of useful contacts at the end of this chapter (pages 68–9).

Rehabilitation: what Government assistance is available?

Remember, when a company is assessing how it can help rehabilitate an employee back to work and how far it would be reasonable to go in making adjustments to assist an employee protected by disability discrimination legislation, extensive Government assistance is available for employers to accommodate disabled employees and job applicants. Also, the availability of financial assistance is a specific factor companies must take into account when considering whether it would be reasonable to make an adjustment under the DDA (see page 23).

Below we summarise the main state funded schemes. Also, financial assistance may be available from charitable organisations although this is an issue outside the scope of this publication.

Disability Employment Advisers

Employers can contact Disability Employment Advisers ('DEA's) through their local job centre, or through Jobcentre Plus. DEAs provide advice on specialist equipment and other ways of accommodating the needs of disabled people. DEAs also have specialist knowledge of the Access to Work Scheme (see below).

More information relating to DEAs is at www.jobcentreplus.gov.uk/cms. asp?Page=/Home/Employers/DisabilityServiceshelpforEmployers

Access to Work Scheme

The Access to Work Scheme ('the AWS'), run by the Employment Service, can significantly help with the extra employment costs of employing a disabled person. For example, under the AWS an employer may be able to receive contributions towards the cost of an adapted keyboard for a person with impaired manual function, or alterations to lifts to accommodate an employee who requires a wheelchair. The level of funding available to an employer depends upon the employment status of the disabled individual at the time of the application. So, for an employee who has been with their employer for six weeks or longer, the programme will pay 80% of approved costs up to £10,000 and 100% of approved costs over and above £10,000 (but the scheme will not make any contribution to costs below £300). The scheme will also pay 100% of all approved travel to work costs.

There are Access to Work Business Centres throughout the country, which can be contacted directly by employers. Addresses, telephone numbers and contact details are available online at www.jobcentreplus.gov.uk/cms.asp?Page=/Home/Employers/DisabilityServiceshelpforEmployers/AccesstoWork. Alternatively, employers can apply for support by contacting their DEA (see page 66).

Workstep

The Workstep Scheme enables employers to give work opportunities to severely disabled people who face more complex burriers to getting or keeping a job. The Scheme is managed by Jobcentre Plus but is essentially a three way partnership between employer, disabled person and Workstep adviser. The Workstep adviser can assist employers to identify any necessary support available, for example through the AWS. Interested employers should contact their DEA in the first instance (see page 66).

New Deal for Disabled People

New Deal for Disabled People aims to help people with disabilities or long term illness to get back into work, or keep work that they are at risk of losing. Job Brokers are available to provide advice to employers on how to adapt the workplace to enable recruitment or retention of a person with a disability and can also offer practical help such as advising on the Government's AWS. Employers interested in making contact with a New Deal Job Broker can contact the New Deal for Disabled Persons Helpline on 0800 137 177 or obtain further information from their local jobcentre or Jobcentre Plus.

WorkCare

WorkCare is a Government funded research initiative designed to test innovative rehabilitation and return to work services. At the time of writing, it is operating in two pilot regions – Birmingham and West Kent/South London. To be eligible, the employee must have: (i) been absent from work for between 6 weeks and 6 months; (ii) have a job to return to; (iii) live and work within one of the two pilot regions; and (iv) be at risk of not returning to work in the foreseeable future because of ill health. Following an assessment by an occupational health doctor, an occupational health nurse will work with the individual to overcome any occupational barriers to their return to work. All services provided by WorkCare are fully funded by the Department for Works and Pensions. WorkCare can be contacted on 020 8255 8182 or online at www.workcare.co.uk

Further contacts

Society of Occupational Medicine

The Society of Occupational Medicine maintains a list of occupational physicians who are available for work. For a fee, you can request details of occupational health physicians in your region. The particular advantage the Society offers is the opportunity for an employer's requirements to be targeted at the right group of specialists from the start.

Information is available on SOM's website: www.som.org.uk.

NHS Plus

Some NHS Trusts are able to sell occupational health support services to small and medium enterprises through NHS Plus, a network of NHS Occupational Health Departments which provide services to non-NHS employers. To join the network, occupational health units agree to work to NHS quality standards. In addition, the NHS Plus website provides information and support to employers and employees. The website address is www.nhsplus. nhs.uk Companies should bear in mind that this service is in its early stages and is not yet available in all regions.

Association of Chartered Physiotherapists in Occupational Health

This organisation can provide contact details of physiotherapists with experience in occupational health for your local area. Contact details are:

The Cottage, Hornsea Road, Atwick, Driffield, East Yorkshire, YO25 8DG

Tel: 0196 453 4376

jslsda@aol.com

The Employers' Forum on Disability

This organisation provides guidance and publications on the employment of, and the business case for, employing disabled people. Contact details are:

Nutmeg House, 60 Gainsford St, London SE1 2NY

Tel: 020 7403 3020

www.employers-forum.co.uk

Focus on rehabilitation

Introduction

◼ What is rehabilitation?

Rehabilitation is a phrase that covers a range of measures, such as a medical intervention or changes to working arrangements or the workplace that helps an absent employee to return to work. It can also enable an employee who is still working but suffering from a chronic illness to be more effective at work.

> The aims of the rehabilitation measures set out in this Guide are:
>
> - to avoid unnecessary sickness absence, ill-health early retirements and dismissals on grounds of capability none of which are in either the employer's or the employee's interests
>
> - to help the employee work (or, if absent, return to work) at his or her highest skill/ability level and do so quickly, and
>
> - to help employees retain or regain their confidence, motivation and relationship with their co-workers and manager.

◼ The business case for rehabilitation

Typically, short-term self-certificated absences account for most spells of absence but long-term absences account for most of the total days lost. It is not uncommon in the manufacturing sector for short-term absences to account for roughly 80 % of spells but long-term absences account for about 80 % of time lost. It is, therefore, the long-term sickness absences that usually cause the greatest financial cost to the business. Effective rehabilitation can significantly reduce that cost.

There are, though, other compelling reasons to consider rehabilitation measures:

- There is a large degree of overlap between rehabilitation measures and the measures employers have a legal duty to take, if it is reasonable to do so, under disability discrimination legislation to enable disabled employees to stay in, or return to, work (see pages 20–24). Employers who do not take on board the requirements of the DDA are exposed to claims for unlimited compensation.

- Unfortunately, given the complexity of the definition of a disability under the legislation (see page 85), it may not always be easy to spot who is covered – until a tribunal decides with the benefit of hindsight. This means a prudent employer should ensure good rehabilitation practices are entrenched in the company so that it has a better chance of meeting its obligations under the DDA in the less obvious cases.

- Some insurers in the UK are now building a requirement for rehabilitation practices into employers' liability insurance policies.

  There are often long waiting lists for services central to rehabilitation such as physiotherapy, counselling, appointments with hospital consultants or for medical investigations and the cost of private healthcare is beyond the reach of most employees. For this reason, there may be justification in some cases, compared with the cost of sick pay, for a company to pay for treatment if it will speed up recovery or result in medical investigations taking place earlier (see pages 90–93).

● Isn't it simpler for the employee to stay off sick?

Yes, it could be from the viewpoint of individual line managers who are inevitably at the centre of initiatives to encourage more rehabilitation. Yet successful initiatives to reduce unnecessary sickness absence (both long and short-term) have an immediate impact on profitability (see the case study on page 7). The aim of all of the initiatives in this Guide is to shift a business away from a 'sick note culture' to a culture of positively managing attendance, including long-term absences. The problem of reluctant managers is considered in more detail on pages 112–14.

Benefits of early intervention

For most employers, musculoskeletal disorders and stress/mental health issues are the main causes of long-term absence. These are conditions for which it is particularly important to begin rehabilitation at the earliest opportunity to prevent them becoming chronic.

The evidence also confirms that the longer an employee is off work, the less likely he or she is to return to working for their employer or, indeed, to stay in the labour market. For example, an employee off work for 6 months has only a 50% chance of returning to work; at 12 months absence the likelihood of returning to work is about 25% and by 2 years of absence, the prospects of successfully returning to work are virtually nil.

Wouldn't we just be opening the floodgates to unmanageable requests for special treatment?

In this Guide we aim not only to illustrate what rehabilitation measures are possible and how they can benefit a company but also to guide employers on managing the process. We know that, for a mixture of reasons, some companies are wary of 'opening the flood-gates' to requests for what might be considered special treatment.

For example, line managers are often reluctant to accommodate changes to the normal shift pattern. There can be good business reasons for this; it can be complicated to implement or manage a one-off change and the supervisor might still have to bring in agency staff to cover the other shifts of someone who has switched to a single shift on a rehabilitation programme. It may also be an issue which is highly emotive for co-workers or, at least, managers fear it will be (although, more commonly, co-workers welcome efforts made to accommodate a sick colleague).

In our experience employment tribunals take a dim view of an employer who has failed to make a reasonable adjustment under the DDA or failed to consider rehabilitation measures before dismissing an employee on the grounds of incapability because they fear setting a precedent. Employment tribunals do not normally accept such speculation as a good enough reason for an employer failing to make adjustments under disability discrimination legislation. Instead there has to be a sound business reason.

This means that, as with all the rehabilitation measures suggested in this Guide, whether or not the company should offer rehabilitation in a particular case is a business decision. Even where employees are protected under the DDA, the employer's obligation is to make only reasonable adjustments taking into account, for example, the extent to which it is practicable for the company to make the adjustment.

Suppose, for example, an occupational health adviser has recommended (with the employee and his or her GP's support) a rehabilitation programme of adjusted duties which also means that the employee is not required to participate in a rotating shift arrangement. The employer is not required to implement the programme (or parts of it) if it could show that to do so would have a disproportionate effect on the running of the business. This might be the case if there was already a number of employees on adjusted duties and the employer was having genuine (as opposed to merely perceived) difficulty in staffing the shifts. It may be impracticable to hire agency workers or to recruit part-time short-term employees with the right skills, training and experience to fill the gap.

In such cases, it may be reasonable not to make the adjustment even if the company has made allowances for many employees in the past if it can show on good business grounds that it cannot absorb another request. As the chances of litigation may be high where an employee has seen other employees benefit from an adjustment, it would be wise to take advice before refusing the request in order to ensure that the business case is sound enough to withstand scrutiny by an employment tribunal.

● Wouldn't rehabilitation just increase pressure on colleagues?

In the short-term this may be the case but some contribution to the team by an employee who would otherwise be absent is often better than none. Furthermore, employee relations are enhanced if employees see their sick or injured colleagues being treated well. They receive the positive message that, if they suffered similar health problems, the company – and their colleagues – would help them too (see also the case study on page 7).

◼ Wouldn't colleagues just see rehabilitation as unfair special treatment?

On occasions employees may feel disgruntled and consider that their colleague has gained special treatment or an unwarranted advantage (for example, if the employee has been excused the obligation to work rotating shifts). The risk of this can be minimised if the employer is seen to be actively managing the rehabilitation programme and regularly reviewing the arrangements. Also, if the employer has previously explained to the workforce the background to the initiatives, it will be easier for them to accept it when it is applied to one of their immediate colleagues.

If the employer detects that colleagues are resentful or sceptical about the rehabilitation arrangements for an employee, then it must manage the situation and diffuse it. This is especially important if the employee is protected under the DDA because if that employee is subjected to any detrimental treatment from colleagues (or any manager) for a reason relating to the disability (such as rehabilitation arrangements), then the employer is very likely to be liable in damages for any distress the employee experiences. Also, the employer should ensure that it keeps confidential from other employees the employee's medical information.

Rehabilitation in practice

In the following sections we consider:

- a case management approach for effective rehabilitation (see pages 75–80)

- recommendations for when to start the rehabilitation process (see pages 80–85)

- typical or 'generic' rehabilitation measures, that is, those that can be applied to a wide range of conditions (see pages 86–90) and in case

studies 2 and 3 (pages 134–42) we consider how they might apply to
two common problems – lower back pain and a stress disorder, and

- the practical and legal issues involved in handling individual cases,
  including obtaining medical reports and managing a rehabilitation
  programme (pages 93–111).

We summarise the process for handling employees with medical conditions
or injuries that are affecting their ability to work in a flowchart on pages
76–7.

Case management

● Adopting a flexible case management approach

Traditionally, and in larger companies in particular, there has been a
tendency for long-term ill health absence to be managed through written
polices which identify trigger points for key steps such as when to contact or
consult employees or obtain medical evidence.

One of the benefits of 'triggers' is that they can help to ensure consistency of treatment (important in avoiding successful unfair dismissal and
discrimination cases) but only as long as the personnel function oversees or
enforces the timetable.

Increasingly, though, there is a view that an over-reliance on triggers
can prevent effective early rehabilitation – employers may miss the boat
for effective interventions such as physiotherapy and counselling which can
prevent acute conditions becoming chronic. Triggers can also result in a passive
response to long-term absence rather than active management and leave
managers feeling frustrated that they cannot take appropriate steps earlier.

Rather than rely only on rigidly defined triggers, EEF advocates that
employers use a case management approach which allows for each case to
be managed on its own facts and to a more flexible timetable. However, it
is also important to specify, as a safety net, time periods by when management action (such as, consultation meetings, requests for medical reports,
etc) should be taken if it has not already been.

We consider how employers can build a case management approach
into their existing policies on pages 130–34.

Handling medical cases: a line manager's guide (see page 78 for notes)

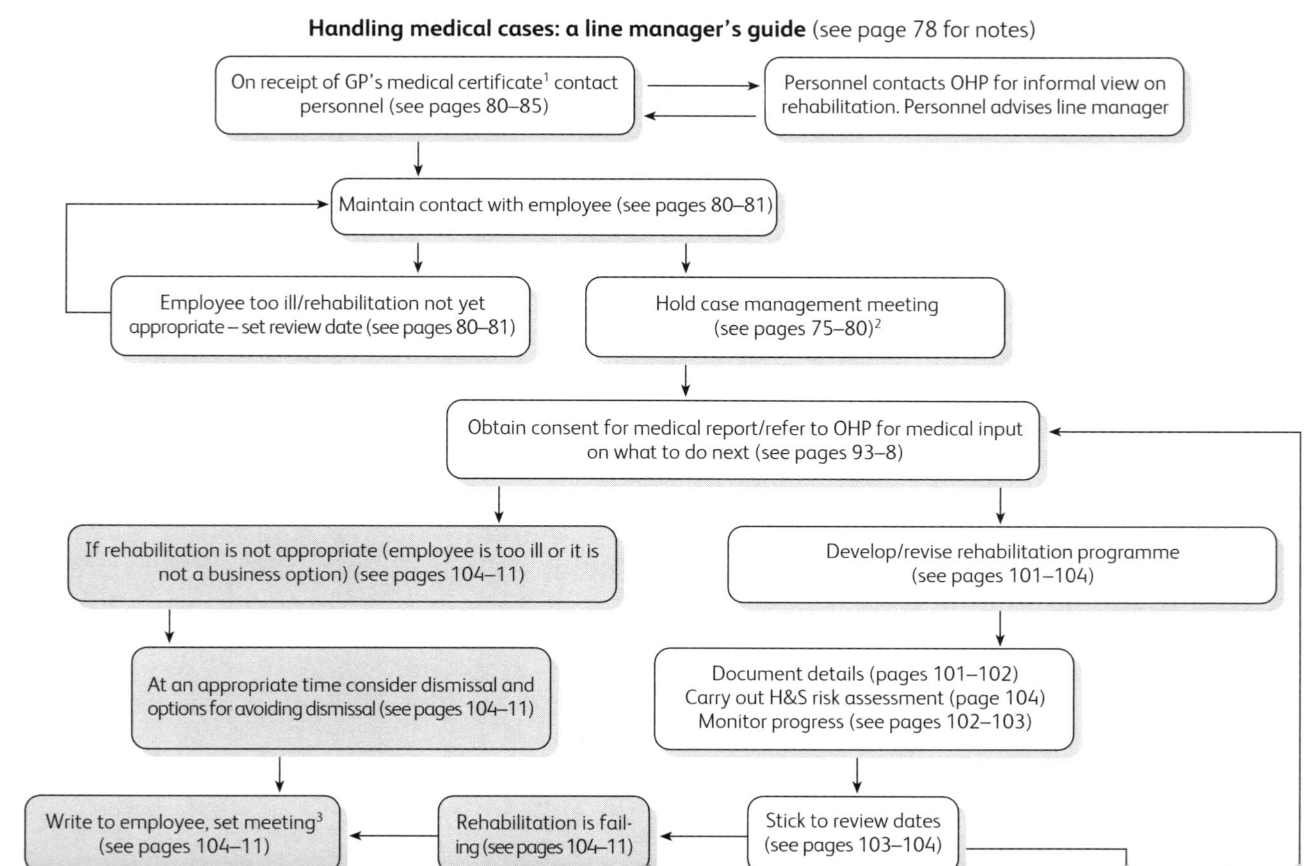

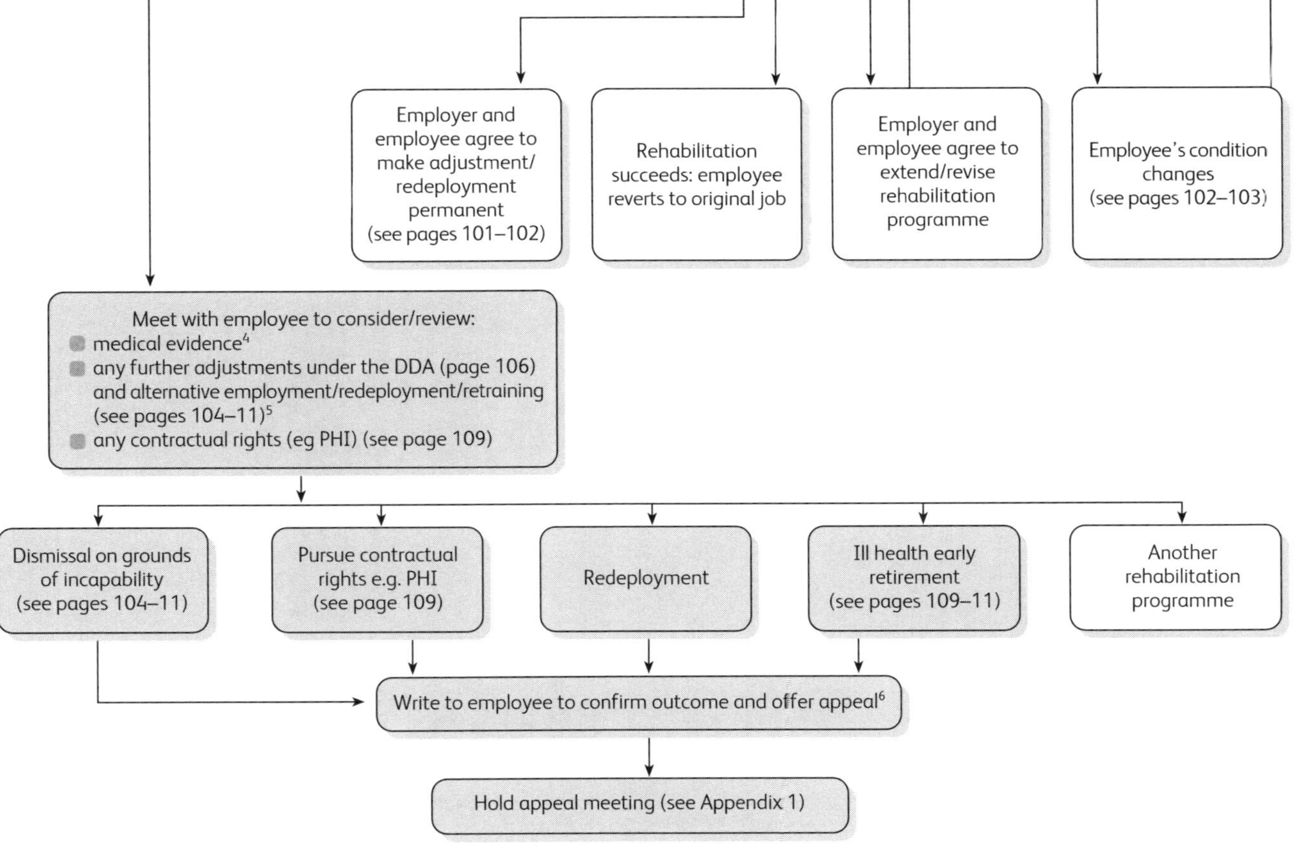

Employer and employee agree to make adjustment/ redeployment permanent (see pages 101–102)
Rehabilitation succeeds: employee reverts to original job
Employer and employee agree to extend/revise rehabilitation programme
Employee's condition changes (see pages 102–103)
Meet with employee to consider/review:
medical evidence[4]
any further adjustments under the DDA (page 106) and alternative employment/redeployment/retraining (see pages 104–11)[5]
any contractual rights (eg PHI) (see page 109)
Dismissal on grounds of incapability (see pages 104–11)
Pursue contractual rights e.g. PHI (see page 109)
Redeployment
Ill health early retirement (see pages 109–11)
Another rehabilitation programme
Write to employee to confirm outcome and offer appeal[6]
Hold appeal meeting (see Appendix 1)

Notes to flow chart on pages 76–7

Note: certain stages in the flowchart are shaded to indicate that, once that stage is reached, there are specific legal issues to bear in mind. These are summarised on pages 104–11.

1. Rehabilitation measures and/or the requirement to make reasonable adjustments under the DDA apply equally to employees who are not yet off sick but who nevertheless have a chronic medical condition or where a medical issue is revealed following a short-term absence.

2. It is preferable to hold a meeting with the employee and his or her companion/representative (see pages 80–81) rather than attempt to cover all of the relevant issues in correspondence.

3. These are mandatory steps under the statutory discipline and dismissal procedure effective from 1 October 2004 and they apply to dismissals and all action short of dismissals (save for warnings/cautions/paid suspension) on the grounds of capability/conduct (see pages 27–31). In summary the steps are:

- write to the employee before taking any action setting out the reasons for the action
- hold a meeting with the employee
- notify the employee in writing of the outcome
- give the employee a right of appeal.

4. It is very likely the employer will need to obtain a supplementary medical report where:

- the initial medical report is stale
- the employer knows or ought reasonably to know that the employee has protection under the DDA, and/or
- new employment issues have come up (for example, a vacancy arises and the employer needs to assess whether the employee is fit enough to do it).

5. If the employer has followed the recommendations for exploring rehabilitation set out in this Guide the employer is very likely to have met already by this stage its legal duty under the DDA to consider reasonable adjustments and consider alternatives to dismissal under unfair dismissal legislation. However, we recommend specifically checking that the employer has complied. Remember too that the duty to consider reasonable adjustments under the DDA is an ongoing one and, for example, a new redeployment opportunity may have arisen since the last time that option was explored.

6. Where the outcome is dismissal or action short of dismissal (other than a warning/caution or paid suspension) the employer must offer a right of appeal. Action short of dismissal includes demotion/redeployment but at the time of writing it is not fully clear what is covered under the new dispute resolution legislation (see pages 27–31). It is safest, therefore, to offer a right of appeal until this aspect of the law is settled as a failure to offer an appeal can render a dismissal automatically unfair and/or lead to an increase in compensation in cases where an aggrieved employee makes a complaint about the outcome under, for example, the DDA.

What is a case management approach?

By a case management approach we mean a co-ordinated effort, at an early stage, between those people in a company that have responsibility for managing the employee and those advising them. The objective is to reduce the amount of time wasted in handling a case caused by poor communication and to ensure that all those who have a role to play in getting an employee back to productive work as quickly as his or her health allows are involved as early as possible in the process. In many companies this will mean an early meeting between the line manager, a representative from the personnel function, the employee and, if appropriate (see page 31), his or her representative. They should meet to consider 'in the round' all relevant aspects of the situation; the needs of the individual, the team and the department as well as the medical advice (if available yet) and, where appropriate, the input of a health and safety adviser. For those companies without a personnel function, the line manager may need to draw on the support of a more senior manager (see pages 38–9). For the reasons considered on pages 122–9 it is preferable that the input on the employee's medical condition and the prospects for rehabilitation should come from an occupational health adviser and not just from the employee's GP or specialist.

A focus on rehabilitation may be more demanding on line managers' time but it pays dividends. Research also suggests that the prospects of accommodating a disabled employee in a particular workplace are enhanced if employers take a cross-departmental or case management approach, thereby reducing their exposure to successful claims under the DDA. Trying to encourage active rehabilitation may not succeed the first time it is tried but the likelihood increases with subsequent cases as employees, managers, occupational health advisers and GPs become more aware of what the business can do (see also the case study on page 7).

Making a case management approach work successfully

A case management approach will be successful if:

- managers are trained to give them the confidence to consider cases according to individual circumstances and to recognise that rehabilitation, for example, may be an appropriate option in cases where an employee has not yet taken sick leave

- managers are proactive in maintaining contact with an employee from the beginning of an absence (see below, pages 80–81)

- all employees are made aware of how such cases will be handled before they go off sick (see pages 56–60)

- the company has access to good occupational health advice (see para 16) and managers consider with their occupational health advisers early on in an absence whether (and if so, to whom) a referral for a full health assessment would be beneficial, and

- senior management and/or the personnel function ensure line managers proactively handle cases rather than waiting until, say, sick pay runs out (see pages 35–6).

When to start the rehabilitation process

- ### Maintaining contact with employees from the start of an absence

Simply staying in contact with the employee is very important, as it is aids recovery and improves the prospects of a speedier return to work. Maintaining contact is the start of the rehabilitation process and it should start as soon as the employee goes off sick. It is preferable to meet the employee to maintain contact but a phone call will suffice if a meeting is not practical.

An employer that establishes and maintains contact with an employee early on in an absence is also more likely to fulfil its requirements under unfair dismissal and discrimination legislation to consult with the employee about the condition and consider alternatives to dismissal.

Many managers wrongly believe that, because an employee is covered by a medical certificate, the employee is off limits and should not be contacted at all. This is not so but it is important that an employer is clear about the purpose of the contact, at whatever stage, to avoid confusion and misunderstanding:

- There will be cases where the possibilities for rehabilitation can be explored at the very beginning of an absence. This may be the case where the employee has back pain or other muscle or joint problems.

- In other cases, the diagnosis or prognosis may be unclear and so any initial contact is simply for the purposes of keeping in touch, to maintain morale and confidence. This may be the case where an employee has gone off sick with stress.

- In yet other cases, it will be clear that the employee is very sick. Initial contact is primarily for welfare purposes and to show that you care.

Consideration of rehabilitation measures is a fluid process because it requires input from a number of participants – the line manager, the personnel function, the occupational health adviser, etc. There may or may not be a clear distinction between simply keeping in touch and active consultation over rehabilitation measures. As long as good notes are kept of all conversations this should not matter.

On the other hand, a meeting or phone call to maintain contact and/or consider rehabilitation with the employee should not be confused with, and should be kept separate from, a consultation meeting about the employee's continued employment where dismissal is being actively considered because rehabilitation is not possible or because the measures are failing (see pages 104–11).

Wouldn't contacting the sick employee be seen as harassment?

It is crucial for managers to stay in contact with an absent employee. There is a myth that contacting an absent employee may be seen as harassment. The vast majority of employees who are sick really appreciate contact from their line manager and their colleagues. Of course, there may be cases where routine contact, at least initially, may be inappropriate. That this is so emphasises why a case management approach to rehabilitation is important so managers can receive early advice from an occupational health adviser and so avoid blundering.

Also, employees are less likely to be hostile to the employer maintaining contact if they are told in advance that this is the approach the company takes. This is another reason why we recommend employers involve their employees and their representatives in the adoption of the initiatives set out in this Guide (see pages 56–60).

Where the company decides that it will review existing cases of employees on long-term sickness absence, it would be beneficial to write to those employees explaining what is about to happen and why. It will then be clearer to them that they are not being singled out for special treatment.

▪ When to actively consider rehabilitation

If, as we recommend, a company deals with long-term absences on a case by case basis, supported by guidelines for when and how action should be taken, to ensure consistency of treatment a line manager should take action on receipt of the first medical certificate. What steps are then taken depends, of course, on its content but, as a general rule of thumb, we suggest the following:

First medical certificate indicates a lengthy absence

The line manager should kick-start the case management process. This means referring the case to whoever has been designated to liaise with the occupational health professional, be that person an external or an in-house adviser. Normally it would be the personnel function who contacts the occupational health professional for an informal view on the likely prognosis and what might be feasible for a return to work (or, where the member company does not have a dedicated personnel officer, a specified manager who has received relevant training (which EEF can provide)). This information will help the manager when he or she contacts the employee.

Succession of medical certificates

Typically this may include cases of lower back pain or stress disorders.

Where, on initial consultation, a GP is not able to give a diagnosis or prognosis, it is standard practice to ask the employee to come for a second consultation in two weeks time. In many cases, this initial two-week absence is enough for recovery and the employee returns to work. In other cases, it is only after the second consultation that the GP will trigger a referral for further investigation or longer-term treatment. The GP may sign the employee off work for another relatively short period, say two weeks or possibly a month.

In these circumstances, we recommend that the line manager seeks at least an informal view from an occupational health adviser on receipt of the first medical certificate and specifically asks the question:

'given what is on the medical certificate, and what the employee has told us, when would it be appropriate to consider rehabilitation measures?'

On the basis of his or her experience, the occupational health adviser may be well placed to give a view on the likely course of an absence for the particular reason given on the medical certificate. For example, he or she may say that it is highly likely that the company will receive a further medical certificate. Furthermore, he or she may suggest that, for that condition, it would be worthwhile contacting the employee straightaway to discuss rehabilitation measures. Alternatively, the message may be, 'wait and see if there is another medical certificate' or 'contact now would be too intrusive and, possibly, exacerbate the employee's condition'. For example, it usually takes about two weeks for an employee and his or her GP to establish how seriously ill an employee is who has been signed off sick with anxiety, stress or depression.

Generally speaking though, consultation with the employee on rehabilitation measures should begin after receipt of the second medical certificate or after a month's absence, whichever is the shorter, unless the company is advised differently by its occupational health adviser.

■ Consultation with employee about rehabilitation

Although the first contact may be by phone, the manager should then organise a meeting with the employee, at a convenient location, most probably a home visit to discuss the possibilities for rehabilitation. Alternatively, the company may want to consider offering to pay taxi fares to help the employee to come to work for a meeting or arrange to meet at a neutral location such as a café or hotel.

The employer should always explain in writing in advance the purpose of any consultation meeting. This means that any letter should make clear that the purpose of the meeting is to explore the options for getting back to work, and to obtain the employee's consent for further medical investigations, if that is appropriate.

This sort of consultation meeting should not be delegated to the personnel function otherwise one of the benefits of a case management approach, cutting down on unnecessary loops in communication between all the parties, will be lost. The line manager should lead the meeting although we recommend that a line manager should always be accompanied when conducting home visits. If there is no personnel officer then another manager should attend, too. Also, as it may not always be clear whether the statutory right to be accompanied may apply (see page 31 for a discussion on determining when this right applies in cases of ill-health), companies should routinely invite employees who are visited at home to be accompanied too, either by a colleague or their trade union representative or other workplace representative.

It would not normally be appropriate for the occupational health adviser to attend as there is a risk of the workforce thinking that the occupational health practitioner is no longer impartial and confidential.

Asking the right questions of the employee

The key to successful rehabilitation is asking the right questions early on. Questions like: 'when will you be fit to return to work?' are useful for a short-term absence of a few days or a week or two but not very useful for someone on long-term sickness absence. This is because it is the GP who will normally decide how long the absence lasts (although this decision can be based on little or no evidence-based medicine (see pages 117–19). Better questions to ask are:

- 'is there anything we (the business) can do to help?'

- 'are you on the waiting list for any treatments, appointments or investigations?' and/or

- 'what might help you to return to work?'

Try to establish exactly what is preventing the employee from returning to work – is it stamina (if so, the employee might be able to do reduced hours), or posture (the employee may not be able to sit or stand for long or have difficulty walking), or concentration? This will help identify what modifications are worth considering.

It may also be appropriate at this early stage to obtain the employee's consent for further medical advice (see pages 93–8).

● **If we ask too many questions, the company might find out the employee has a disability. Isn't this unwise?**

On the contrary, it is unwise not to ask questions because:

● The DDA Code of Practice (see page 18) states that an employer must do all that It can reasonably be expected to do to find out whether an employee has a disability.

● In any event, as in so many cases which have already gone to tribunal, an employment tribunal piecing together who knew what, might, with the benefit of hindsight, hold that the employer already knew enough to be on notice that the employee might have a qualifying disability. In such cases, the duty to make reasonable adjustments still applies even if the employer has not been expressly told of a disability (see page 21).

● Even if the employee is not disabled, consultation with an employee about the prognosis for a return to work is a crucial ingredient of a fair dismissal process (see pages 24–6). A decision to dismiss on grounds of capability will not be fair unless the employer takes into account all the relevant facts that are known or could reasonably be discovered at the time of the dismissal.

Next steps

As with all conversations/meetings, what happens next depends on what emerges at the consultation meeting together with any advice received from the occupational health professional advising the company. It may be:

- Wait and see. In which case, fix a review date.

- Refer to the occupational health adviser or company-appointed medical specialist for an assessment including the possibilities for rehabilitation. In our view, companies should automatically be referring for occupational health advice employees who have had one month's absence unless there is a clear reason to vary this (such as the timetable for a major operation. Even in such cases, there may be some scope for rehabilitation even if it is just staying in touch (see page 87).

- Approach the employee's GP/specialist for a medical report, again, addressing the possibilities for rehabilitation. The company will need the employee's consent to obtain this type of report (see pages 93–8).

If the company does not already have an occupational health service to ask about a rehabilitation programme, it could refer to the suggestions for accessing support set out in Step 4. Alternatively, the employer will need to contact the GP. However, we suggest employers should rely only on the employee's GP input as a last resort. A GP's primary function is to act as an advocate for the patient and so the employer should generally seek advice on its own account.

It should be remembered that, if an employer dismisses an employee without having an adequate picture of his or her current condition and the likely prognosis, an employment tribunal is very likely to find the dismissal unfair. Medical evidence is also very likely to be useful when a company is deciding whether any reasonable adjustments could be made to enable a disabled employee to return to work.

Typical rehabilitation measures

● Introduction

In this section we consider 'generic' rehabilitation measures, that is, those that can be applied to a wide range of conditions. We consider on pages 101–102 and 127–9 some of the knock-on effects to employees' terms and conditions and other practical issues.

■ Encourage visits to the workplace to 'keep in touch'

The value of this cannot be overstated. By allowing the employee to maintain contact with the workplace, it helps to maintain or build the employee's confidence about returning to work. It also encourages dialogue about arrangements for returning to work.

The window of opportunity for a high success rate for rehabilitation is around 4–6 weeks of absence. Any interventions that will allow an employee to begin rehabilitation around this 4–6 week window are worth pursuing even if the intervention is just keeping in regular contact with the employee or just getting the employee to visit the workplace 'for a cup of tea'.

■ Allow a phased return to work

This is a cornerstone of rehabilitation. It recognises that people are not totally sick one day and fully fit the next and that employees often feel more tired than usual when they first start back to work.

A rehabilitation programme based on a phased return to work for an employee normally working full-time might mean the employee initially working:

- 2–4 hours a day,
- 5 hours on alternative days, or
- 1 or 2 full days a week.

For some employees, working 5 short or half days would be less beneficial than, say, 2 full days because of the amount of travel or the type of work being undertaken. Also, allowing employees to work their reduced hours period before and after lunch allows the employee to take advantage of a natural break to the work. Employers should also take into account practical factors that could affect start and finish times such as travel arrangements.

■ Alter the pattern of work

This refers to simplifying working patterns if an employee is required to work shifts. For example, moving the employee from night to day shift or staying with a particular shift pattern rather than rotating.

■ Alter the employee's tasks or work content

This could involve simplifying the range of work activities (for example, initially the employee takes telephone messages but does not deal directly with customers' inquiries (or complaints)). Larger businesses may have the option of temporarily transferring the employee to another job.

■ Adapt the workplace

This option may include:

- making adaptations to the building (for example, installing a hand rail or banister for stairs)

- changing the site of the employee's workstation (for example, moving it to the ground floor for someone with difficulty walking up stairs), or

- altering the layout of an employee's work area – this is particularly important to consider when rehabilitating employees with musculoskeletal disorders (bones, joints or muscle problems).

■ Reduce the pace of work

This could mean temporarily reducing the employee's exposure to difficult targets and deadlines or allowing the employee to have more frequent or longer breaks. This may be difficult to accommodate on certain production lines but it is advisable to actively consider such suggestions before concluding that they are not feasible. Remember that, when considering a claim under the DDA, an employment tribunal can closely scrutinise the merits of the business case put forward by the employer seeking to establish that a particular adjustment would not be reasonable. This means the employer must check before, say, dismissing on grounds of medical incapacity that its assumptions hold water. Employees undergoing rehabilitation may also need more assistance than usual in prioritising work.

■ Adapt tools and equipment

Many modifications or adaptations to office furniture, machinery and plant, IT equipment or other work equipment can be made at very low cost. For example, someone with arthritis in the hands can improve their grip strength if their tools have larger diameter handles.

If substantial changes are required, some state funding may be available (see page 66).

● Provide further training or information

This may be necessary so that an employee can continue in their current job. For example, the employee may need specific training on how to carry out aspects of the job affected by their illness or injury such as how to lift or carry without straining, or how to use mechanical aids. Training may also be required to enable employees to transfer to alternative work.

The employer's occupational health adviser can also give employees useful medical information about their condition and dispel common myths as well as identifying when more should be done medically. For example, it is commonly believed that immobility helps people with back problems recover, whereas, the modern view is that staying active is, for many people, beneficial (see further pages 115–17).

● Provide for mobility and transport

This is another cornerstone of a typical rehabilitation programme as mobility and transport problems can often be the main obstacle to a return to work. For example, the employer could:

- allow an employee to park closer to their workplace, or

- if it is difficult for the employee to get to work on public transport, pay for a taxi for an employee to get to work. This is a simple measure that often makes more economic sense than paying the employee company sick pay.

State funding, under the 'Access to work' scheme may also be available (see pages 66–7).

> ■ Further reading: 'Line managers' resource pack' for managing mental health in the workplace
>
> Produced by MindOUT, the Mental Health Foundation, the 'Line managers' resource pack' is a practical guide to managing and supporting mental health in the workplace. It is about the effective management of people with mental health problems. It contains very practical advice on: what to say and do, how to manage an employee who is off sick with mental ill-health and how to plan an effective return to work. There are sections on, for example, engaging with someone who is reluctant to talk, managing an employee who becomes tearful and upset and managing an ongoing illness whilst at work.
>
> EEF has actively contributed to the MindOUT for Mental Health campaign and specifically to the Resource Pack and we recommend it as a useful companion publication to this Guide because it is targeted at line managers. It is available free from the Mental Health Foundation: www.mindout.net or Tel no: 0870 443 0930.

Paying for treatment

■ Should a business pay for treatment or medical investigations?

In 2002, only a month after breaking a bone in his foot, David Beckham was back playing football on the world stage. Most manual employees would have been signed off sick for about 3 months. What made the difference? Prompt, intensive treatment and physiotherapy as well as his own motivation.

Many companies now appreciate that they can cut the length of some absences (and, therefore, the total costs of sickness absence) by organising and paying for early and/or more intensive treatment. In some production jobs an employee may not be fit enough to work even though they have only a minor injury and this may easily be treated by, for example, physiotherapy. There are other, indirect benefits, too, if the employer routes all treatments through one provider. For example, if employees are sent to the same physiotherapist, he or she may be able to spot trends in workplace injuries and be able to feed those back to the company.

Of course, there are a number of options. Some employers provide group private health care cover, on a contributory or a non-contributory basis. Conventionally, this benefit is often reserved for staff employees. However, some companies find it can be a very cost effective benefit to provide for manual employees as it can cut down the length of absences.

Alternatively, the employer can provide on site services. For example, a physiotherapist may attend site once a week or the employer can decide to pay for treatment on an ad hoc basis. The rest of this section is concerned with the latter option.

■ Is payment always in the company's and employee's best interests?

There will be many cases where there is no doubt that it would be cost effective for the company to pay for an employee to have medical treatment. For example, the cost of a private session with a physiotherapist, chiropractor or osteopath (usually around £25 to £30 per session) is a relatively small price to pay to assist someone with say, back pain, or other musculoskeletal disorders, to return to work compared with the cost of sick pay whilst the employee waits for the NHS physiotherapy service or for 'rest' to make things better. Similarly, given the length of NHS waiting lists for MRI scans (often about 3 months), paying privately may progress matters significantly. Typically an MRI scan costs £500–£600.

However, it is wise to take advice from an occupational health physician or nurse when considering paying for treatment or investigations privately. There are situations involving mental health where it is less clear that private intervention will help. Take the example of someone with stress, anxiety or depression. There is evidence that some people will find cognitive behavioural therapy (CBT) very useful and it may facilitate a return to work much earlier than other treatments or rest. However, CBT is relatively expensive (around £1,200 for 6 hours of therapy) and it may not help if there are fundamental problems with the employee's family life, work or physical health unless these are also addressed. Where the employee is suffering mental health problems, the company should definitely seek a medical assessment to help decide whether to pay for private interventions.

■ Ensuring employees are treated equitably when considering paying for treatment

The company should have transparent guidelines or criteria for assessing whether to pay privately for investigations/treatment in each individual case. It should not be left to line managers to exercise a subjective judgment about whether it is appropriate for one employee but not another. This may lead to employee relations problems and suggestions of unfair treatment from those who are not granted the benefit. This may even lead to grievances or cases alleging discrimination. Instead, the decision should be informed by advice from an occupational health adviser which the manager then weighs against the cost and other implications of the employee staying off work.

■ Tax liability

The HSE has recently provided guidance on the tax implications when employers provide occupational health support and/or pay for private treatment (see www.hse.gov.uk/pubns/taxrules.pdf).

The guidance states that, if the employer pays for health-related services or treatments, they are not considered to be an employee benefit (which means the employee is not liable for tax and the employer can claim a deduction against business profits) if they are for:

■ work-related conditions or accidents that are solely caused by work

■ health screening and check-ups

■ welfare counselling

■ equipment and services for disabled workers, or

■ recreational and sporting facilities that are for employees only

provided the employer pays for the treatments or services directly rather than giving or reimbursing the employee the money for them.

So, if the employer pays for private physiotherapy treatment for a condition that is not work-related (such as to deal with a sports injury) then the Inland Revenue is very likely to treat that payment as a taxable benefit.

On the face of it, this may be a significant disincentive for both employer and employee in paying for private treatment and is a factor that employers need to consider when weighing up whether it is in the employer's and employee's interests to pay for the employee's treatment. EEF is lobbying Government to remove this disincentive.

Obtaining medical information

■ Consent to provide medical information

Medical information can be obtained from the employee's own GP or specialist or, preferably, the company may decide to ask its occupational physician or an independent doctor to examine the employee and prepare a report.

Even if the company decides to seek an independent medical assessment, the occupational physician will normally want information from the employee's GP or specialist. A company cannot obtain medical information about an employee, or require an employee to undergo a medical examination, unless the employee consents. Inevitably, this introduces some delay but that can be reduced if the company seeks consent as early as possible. It may be best to ask the employee to give any signed consents in the first consultation meeting (see pages 83–4). Advice on obtaining good quality medical reports is set out on pages 95–6 of this Guide. The employer's obligations under the Access to Medical Reports Act 1988 are set out in paras 3.2.69–3.2.76 of the 2003/04 EEF Employment Guide (www.employmentguide.org.uk) and specimen documentation is also available on that site.

■ Can we force an employee to attend an interview with our own medical advisers?

If the company decides to obtain a report from its own adviser, an employee is perfectly entitled to refuse consent to attend the company's doctor. The company then has no alternative but to make a decision about the management of the employee's absence on the basis of the information that it does have. This should be made clear to an employee who is inclined to refuse consent, but without pressurising him or her to attend. The same applies if the employee refuses consent to the company obtaining information from his or her own doctor.

The contract of employment may contain a clause whereby, on taking up the job, the employee agreed to submit to a medical examination at the company's request. If he or she refuses when asked, technically, the employee is in breach of contract. However, a dismissal on that ground is fraught with difficulty. Also, if the employer puts pressure on the employee to undergo a medical examination this is likely to be grounds for constructive dismissal and it may be so even if the contract contains a clause requiring compulsory medical examination.

We suggest, instead, that the employer continues to follow the guidance on pages 104–11 for dismissals on the grounds of incapability but making a clear record of the attempts to advise the employee of the wisdom of co-operating with the employer's process and of the employee's refusal.

● Can we withhold sick pay if an employee refuses consent to attend the company's doctor?

Whether the employer can withhold company sick pay from an employee who refuses to give consent to attend the company doctor will depend entirely on the terms of the employer's sick pay scheme. For it to be safe from breach of contract/unlawful deduction from wages claims for wrongly withholding company sick pay the contract should expressly provide that company sick pay may be withheld if an employee refuses to co-operate with a request for a medical report or other measures for managing the employee's absence. Also the mandatory procedural rules under the statutory discipline and dismissal procedure will apply from 1 October 2004 (see pages 27–31) to any proposal to withhold sick pay. In summary, this means writing to employees telling them of the reason for withholding sick pay, holding a meeting and giving them a right of appeal (see pages 27–31 for more details).

An employer can only withhold SSP from a qualifying employee on very limited grounds (which are unlikely to apply here) such as when the employer has good grounds to doubt the employee is seriously ill (see the 2003/04 EEF Employment Guide, para 3.2.41, or www.employmentguide.org.uk).

▪ Contacting the employee's GP/specialist

The employer must follow strict rules when seeking medical information from the employee's GP or any other doctor who has had responsibility for the employee's care. These rules are summarised on pages 51–2. To help employers comply with these rules, specimen documentation is available on the EEF Employment Guide website at www.employmentguide.org.uk.

The easiest and most direct way of approaching the GP is to give the employee the employer's request for information. The employee can then hand this, together with a copy of his or her written consent, to the GP at the next consultation. Alternatively, the employee can send it to the surgery in advance of the consultation if the issues are quite complicated and it might be better to give the GP time to consider the issues. Otherwise, if the employer just sends the request to the GP, it may not be dealt with for several weeks (or even months).

If it has not been possible to obtain the employee's written consent to a report in a meeting (for example, if the employee is too ill to attend a consultation meeting with the employer), then the employer will have no alternative but to write to the employee seeking written consent and then send the consent together with the employer's request for information to the doctor.

If the medical report is not received within around 3 weeks of the application to the doctor, contact the doctor's surgery to encourage a response.

Employers should of course expect GPs to charge for preparing a medical report.

Irrespective of how the company sends its request to the GP or the employee's specialist, the employee has the right to see the report before it is sent to the employer and can refuse to give consent for the doctor to send it to the employer (see pages 51–2).

▪ How do we ensure the company receives good quality medical information?

Employers regularly complain that medical reports are unhelpful, don't answer the right questions, etc. There is no doubt that an employer will receive a better quality medical report if it takes care at the outset to ask the right questions. The onus is on the line manager and personnel function to give the doctor enough information and ask detailed questions to ensure that the response is sufficiently good to make informed decisions (see below, pages 96–7). A major reason for having a case management meeting with an employee before writing for a medical report is that the employer is then far better placed to ask specific questions and to give the doctor relevant information about the context of the job. We provide a checklist of issues below.

Employers may need to obtain more than one report as employment decisions should be made on up-to-date medical information. For example, once the employer has received the GP's report, it might commission its own report following consultation with its advisers. It may then be appropriate to ask the GP to comment on that report. Also, if some time has elapsed since a report was first received and rehabilitation is failing, the employer should obtain a supplementary report to guide it in its next steps before deciding whether to dismiss (see pages 104–11).

■ Checklist: what should we include in a request for medical information?

We set out below a checklist of issues to be covered in a request for a medical report. It is important, though, to tailor requests to the circumstances of the particular case. GPs in particular are more likely to respond quickly to a request focused on the patient rather than a wide ranging pro forma.

The request should:

■ explain that the company is reviewing the employee's absence and that it would like to help the employee get back to normal work as soon as possible

■ give the doctor a summary of the employee's actual, current duties (and not what may be written on an out-of-date job description). It may be helpful to refer to some of the following (dependent on the person's job) in compiling the summary:

  – demands of the job (e.g. is it physically/mentally/intellectually challenging?)

- the working environment (e.g. shop floor or office, fumes, dust, chemicals, at heights, walking between buildings, stairs, layout of work area, etc)
- working time issues (e.g. shift working, early start time)
- travel (e.g. any business travel, or to other sites)
- organisational issues (e.g. whether the employee is part of a team or a lone worker, or dealing with customers, etc)

- ask for the doctor's view on whether the employee is fit to do his or her current job. This is best done by asking a targeted question such as 'are there any actual functional problems that are preventing the employee from returning to work, such as:
  - stamina
  - manual handling – difficulty lifting carrying/mobility/dexterity
  - medication (particularly side effects and expected duration)
  - mental state/concentration
  - motivation?'

- ask the doctor if any of the following might facilitate a return to work:
  - allowing a phased return to work
  - reduced hours
  - altering the pattern of work
  - altering or reducing the work content
  - adaptations to the workplace
  - reducing the pace of work
  - adaptations to tools and equipment
  - providing further training, or
  - providing for mobility or transport

  This information will also allow the employer to decide whether the employee could do any alternative jobs that are available.

- tell the GP about the employer's keenness to pursue rehabilitation measures and support the employee returning to work (see further pages 117–19).

● When should we ask for the GP's opinion on when the employee will be fit to return to the original job?

If the employee is not currently fit to do his or her full normal job, it is conventional to ask the GP at the outset, in a first request for a medical report, for his or her opinion on when the employee would be fit to return to it. We suggest employers do not routinely ask this question at this very early stage when the parties are exploring rehabilitation. This is because inevitably GPs will be cautious when answering it. If, for example, the GP was to state 'in 3 months', it may be more difficult for the employee and GP to then agree to a rehabilitation programme starting earlier than this.

If, however, rehabilitation is not appropriate or is started and fails, the employer should ask 'when will the employee be able to return to work in the original job?' when asking for a further report (see pages 107–108).

● Should we now ask the GP's view on whether the employee qualifies under the DDA?

We suggest that, at the initial stages of seeking the GP's view on rehabilitation, employers do not burden GPs with this question. The employer would have to explain the Act's provisions and the GP may well take a cautious approach and say 'yes' or decline to answer it on the basis that it is too early to tell. The question is likely to result in delay when, at this stage, what we suggest employers want most to know is the GP's views on rehabilitation.

In any event, by asking specific questions about what an employee is capable of (as set out on pages 96–7) an employer is very likely to be asking questions which are relevant to its duty under the DDA to make reasonable adjustments.

If, however, the medical evidence suggests rehabilitation is not appropriate or, if a rehabilitation programme is started and fails, the employer should seek further medical evidence before deciding to dismiss and should specifically seek views on whether the employee qualifies under the DDA (see pages 107–108).

Deciding what the company should do next

Assessing all the medical information received

Once the medical information has been received, the company has to assess whether it is sufficient to make an informed decision on the prospects for rehabilitation and/or, if appropriate, the employee's future employment. The report may not address the points that the company has asked it to address or it may be unclear. If so, the company may need to go back to the doctor for further information or clarification.

Remember, the role of medical evidence is to inform the company's decision making, rather than substitute for it. A doctor's opinion on whether an employee is fit to return to work is only one factor that the company will need to take into account when deciding how to manage the employee's case. Likewise, the question of whether an employee is disabled within the definition of the Disability Discrimination Act 1995 is a question of fact, and a doctor's view on this is not conclusive. While a doctor may be able to give valuable input on possible adjustments for a disabled employee, whether a particular adjustment is reasonable in all the circumstances is an assessment for the company to make.

One important consequence of the above is that a tribunal will not allow an employer to hide behind a poorly thought out medical report to defend its failure to make an adjustment, particularly if the adjustment was an obvious one. This puts a tough burden on employers and is another reason why companies need to have good quality occupational health advice in these cases.

What if conflicting medical evidence is received?

Where medical evidence is obtained from more than one source and there is a conflict, the employer should first ask its own medical adviser to try and resolve it or at least narrow down the issues in conflict. This would involve the adviser writing to the employee's GP/specialist.

It is also important for the company to discuss the medical evidence and the conflict with the employee to ensure that any comments that the employee has about its accuracy are taken into account (see pages 100–101).

If the conflict cannot be resolved, the company is entitled to rely on the evidence that it believes to be the most credible, provided it has reasonable grounds for that belief. For example, if the company has obtained a report from an employee's GP and one from its occupational health adviser, it may prefer the occupational health report because that doctor has a better idea of what is involved in the job and the type of working environment in which it is performed.

What are the implications of the medical evidence?

The next step is to hold a case management meeting to consider the implications of the medical evidence. The likely options are:

- rehabilitation/reasonable adjustments (see pages 86–90 and 20–24 respectively), which may involve retraining

- redeployment, which, again, may involve retraining

- dismissal

- ill-health early retirement (see pages 109–11), and

- in exceptional cases, leave to review at a later date (see pages 80–81).

Importance of further consultation with the employee

The next step is to consult with the employee. The purpose of further consultation is three-fold:

- to consult an employee on the medical evidence received. It may contain factual errors or misunderstandings, or be out of date. It is better to find out about these in a consultation meeting rather than an employment tribunal

- to jointly consider with the employee the possible options. It is important that there is a meaningful discussion about the possibilities. If an employer comes to the meeting with a closed mind, that is, with 'decisions' rather than 'proposals', this could be held against the employer in any tribunal proceedings, and

- to ask the employee if he or she has any further suggestions for steps that might enable the employee to return to work.

As with all meetings with employees, careful notes should be taken. The employer should then write to the employee summarising the discussion and recording any agreement reached. If the parties have gone away to consider any points, the letter should make that clear and set a deadline for responding. If the employee has raised suggestions that the employer has not considered before, the employer should take time to investigate them.

Managing a rehabilitation programme

When implementing a rehabilitation programme for individual employees, whether they are on long term sick, are working but have a chronic condition or have a pattern of frequent short-term absence with a suspected underlying cause, there are a number of practical issues to bear in mind which are considered below.

● Properly document the terms of the rehabilitation arrangements

It is vital to record the terms of any agreement reached on rehabilitation or redeployment, be it temporary or permanent because:

- the parties then know where they stand

- there is a legal requirement to inform employees in writing of any changes to their terms and conditions within a month of the change taking place (see pages 58–9), and

- failure to do so simply stores up problems for the future. For example, if an employee undertakes alternative duties temporarily but the situation drifts, with no record or review, there can be serious difficulties in deciding how to treat that employee in a future restructuring or redundancy round.

Many of the issues relating to status and terms and conditions raised by rehabilitation measures (or transfer to permanently restricted duties or redeployment) are dealt with on pages 127–9. Whatever is agreed must be clearly documented to prevent future disputes. Issues to be covered include:

- Is a change in working hours, duties, etc a permanent arrangement or temporary? It is vital that a proper record of the employee's status is kept. This may assist the employer in the event that it wishes to make redundancies by helping to clarify what the employee's substantive post is and, therefore, which pool, if any, the employee should be placed in for the purposes of redundancy selection.

- When are the arrangements to be reviewed? Ensure dates to review arrangements are strictly observed.

- Record the terms of pay protection arrangements. How long will protection or personal red circling last? When is it to be reviewed? If it is long-term, will employees still be entitled to pay awards, to participate in bonuses, performance-related pay, etc?

Permanent pay protection arrangements (that is, where the employee carries out a less well paid role but continues to receive his or her original pay rate and the pay awards for that grade, etc) cause serious long-term employee relations problems such as grievances and equal pay problems and should be avoided.

Monitoring the employee's progress and preventing relapses

Once the company and employee have agreed on rehabilitation measures, and the timescale for them, the company must continue to actively manage that programme to ensure that the employer complies with its duty of care to the employee. This means:

- Holding regular monitoring meetings between employee and line manager to check how the employee is coping and, if necessary, making adjustments to the programme. Initially, these meetings should be weekly then more spaced out once it is clear the programme is going well.

- Arranging for regular meetings between the employee and the occupational health adviser, again to check that the agreed measures and the timescale is still appropriate and that there has not been a change in the employee's clinical condition. If there has, the rehabilitation measures should be reviewed.

So, for example, it may have been agreed that, for a period of a month, the employee would return to work at 50% of normal hours, gradually building up to 100% over another month. At the first weekly meeting with the line manager the employee may feel that he or she has underestimated the impact of coming back to work and so it is agreed that he or she will work only 30% normal hours for a couple of weeks and build up to normal hours more gradually.

The programme should be set out in writing. Any changes to it should be approved by the occupational health adviser and in some circumstances the employee's GP and/or specialist. If the employee is going to undertake different duties for a specified period then this should be recorded which will help clarify the employee's contractual position if rehabilitation takes longer than expected.

Notes should be kept of all monitoring or review meetings.

◼ Can rehabilitation impede an employee's recovery?

Employees rehabilitated into work generally recover faster than those left at home. Also, if the employer follows the advice in this Guide and holds regular monitoring meetings (see above, pages 102–103) then, in the event that the employee is not coping well, further adjustments can be made. This should ensure employees do not overstretch themselves or undertake activities which might impede their recovery.

However, it is important to keep the employee's progress under review and to monitor for any change in the employee's clinical position (see above, pages 102–103).

◼ Stick to review dates

If a company fails to set and/or adhere to reviews of a rehabilitation programme it will be storing up trouble for the future. If a timetable drifts, usually there comes a reason, a restructuring/redundancy or a new line manager's arrival, which prompts the employer to look afresh at the employee's situation. By that time, it may be unclear what the normal job is for the employee, who may be reluctant to return to the original job. It may be difficult without advice to discern what the true contractual position is.

There is often a temptation to take short cuts when re-considering the case because of the time that has elapsed or because there are other pressing circumstances. This may lead to the employer losing a claim under the DDA or unfair dismissal legislation. Take for example, an employee with a disability who was transferred to restricted duties and the employer, one year later, decides that it no longer needs an employee in that role. There is still a duty on the employer to make reasonable adjustments when considering how to treat that employee in the redundancy situation. Employers should, therefore, seek advice before dismissing an employee who has for some time been left, without review, in a rehabilitation-type role.

- Carry out health and safety risk assessments for the adjusted role

If an employee is rehabilitated back into work or redeployed into an alternative role whether on a temporary or permanent basis, it is important to revisit the risk assessment which has previously been done generally for the workforce for that work. This is because a risk assessment must take account of the known vulnerabilities of any particular workers and so the employer must take reasonably practicable precautions under the Health and Safety at Work Act 1974.

What if rehabilitation is not appropriate or fails?

General principles

One of the aims of rehabilitation is to cut down on the number of dismissals and ill-health retirements. There may come a point, though, when the employer concludes it needs to review the employee's continued employment because rehabilitation is not possible or it has been tried but was not successful.

In such cases the employer must also comply with its obligations under:

- unfair dismissal and disability discrimination legislation

- the statutory right to be accompanied which also applies where the employer is considering dismissal or action short of dismissal (such as a demotion or redeployment (see page 31))

- the new statutory minimum procedures for resolving disputes, which come into force on 1 October 2004. These also apply to dismissals and certain types of action short of dismissal on the grounds of ill-health (see pages 27–31). Failure to follow these can result in a finding of automatic unfair dismissal (see page 30).

Summary of legal obligations

In summary, the essential legal obligations are:

- to consult with the employee

- before dismissing, an employee must be made aware in writing, if it is the case, that his or her continued employment is under review (see pages 106–107)

- if the company has one, it should follow its own attendance management procedure (except for any terms that are inconsistent with the statutory procedural rules in which case the particular term of the latter overrides the employer's term (see pages 27–31))

- where appropriate, obtain medical advice or further, up-to-date medical advice (see pages 107–108)

- write to the employee explaining the reason why the employer is proposing to dismiss and inviting the employee to a meeting. At that meeting the employer should (if it has not already done so) consult about any additional medical information received (see pages 100–101) and consult on alternatives to dismissal (including further rehabilitation measures, redeployment and/or retraining) before terminating employment on the grounds of incapability to avoid liability under unfair dismissal and disability discrimination legislation

- write to the employee explaining the employer's decision and the right of appeal (see pages 27–31 and Appendix 1), and

> - observe the statutory right to be accompanied (see page 31).
>
> On pages 106–11 below we consider how the employer can meet the obligations not already considered so far in this Guide.

● Checking that the employer has complied with the DDA

If an employer has followed the advice so far in this Guide, it is very likely to have met its obligations under the DDA and unfair dismissal legislation by consulting the employee on rehabilitation measures, redeployment and retraining and obtaining medical evidence. As we have explained above, in practice there will be a large amount of overlap between standard or generic rehabilitation measures and possible adjustments that should be considered under the DDA. But, as such a high standard is required of an employer under the DDA we advise employers to specifically check off those obligations to make sure they are not missed (see pages 20–24).

Also, the duty to make reasonable adjustments is an ongoing one; circumstances may have changed since rehabilitation/redeployment was first considered. For example, the employee may have tried a phased return to work over a 3-month period to the original job but it has failed. In the meantime, a vacancy has arisen which, with reasonable adjustments, the employee might be suitable for. This should be considered and, if necessary, the employer should obtain a further medical report to help it assess suitability.

● Ensuring the employer warns employees that dismissal may be an outcome and complying with the statutory disciplinary and dismissal and grievance procedures

It is a basic principle of unfair dismissal law that an employee should be made aware before dismissal that termination of employment is an option the employer is considering.

Employers, therefore, have to decide when to make this clear to an employee. This is not so difficult when an employer only starts to consider the future employment prospects once an individual has been away sick for some time. It is more difficult if employers are following the advice advocated in this Guide, that is, maintaining contact with the employee and actively consulting on the possibilities for rehabilitation at a very early stage in an absence. Warning employees at the outset that, if rehabilitation is not possible, or if it is unsuccessful, they may be dismissed would appear hasty and send them the wrong signal. It would also be inappropriate if the employee has the benefit of a generous sick pay scheme.

On the other hand, if, after initial consultation to explore rehabilitation, the employer concludes dismissal is the only option, then it risks a finding of automatic unfair dismissal if it has not explained in writing that is what it is considering before it dismisses and if it does not follow the other procedural steps summarised on pages 27–31. Under these statutory procedural rules the employer is required to give the employee written notice of its intentions and the grounds for the action it proposes, and to hold a meeting with the employee about them (see pages 27–31).

Employers must make it clear and in writing when the process of exploring rehabilitation has expired and active consideration of dismissal or permanent redeployment to another post (as opposed to temporary redeployment for the purposes of rehabilitation) has begun. Under the statutory minimum discipline and dismissal procedure they must also hold a meeting with the employee, write to him or her to explain the outcome and, again in writing, offer an appeal against the outcome.

◼ Ensuring the company has sufficient medical evidence

There will be cases where, at the outset, the prognosis for rehabilitation is poor or a rehabilitation programme does not succeed and the employee goes back off sick. In order to protect itself from unfair dismissal and/or disability discrimination cases, it is important that the company can demonstrate that it:

- took medical advice rather than made an assumption about the prognosis or the reason for the failure of the rehabilitation, whichever is the case, and

- consulted the employee about that advice.

If the employer has already sought medical advice on rehabilitation it may have met this obligation. It may be, though, that the advice is old in which case we suggest that a further medical report be sought. In contrast with earlier requests for medical reports (see page 98) we suggest employers specifically ask the doctor to give an opinion on when the employee is likely to return to the original job or to any type of work and, if so, what and when.

The request should also ask the doctor for an opinion on whether the employee meets the definition of a disability under the DDA. The doctor should specifically be invited to decline to answer that question if they are unsure otherwise they may, out of caution, say yes. Of course, the doctor's view is not conclusive of the question whether the employee is disabled but it is helpful for the employer to know the doctor's opinion.

If they are asked to give an opinion they should also be asked to give examples of how the disability affects the employee's ability to carry out day-to-day activities and be referred to the guidance on what qualifies as a disability[10] (see page 17). Contact an EEF Association for advice on the letter's contents if required.

The employer should also specifically ask the employee: 'Is there anything further we can do?' Employees should be consulted about any additional medical reports too.

■ Deciding on dismissal

In some cases, the medical information will confirm that the employee is unlikely to return to work within a reasonable time or that the prognosis for rehabilitation is poor. Even if the prognosis is not poor it may not be reasonable on business grounds to allow the employee to return to amended or alternative duties. Alternatively, the employee may have started on a rehabilitation programme only for his or her condition to have changed or for the rehabilitation programme to be unsuccessful for some other reason.

In these circumstances, the company will, therefore, need to decide

---

10 The Government has issued guidance on the definition of a disability. It gives extensive examples on when an impairment should, or should not, be viewed as having a substantial effect on a person's day-to-day activities. 'Guidance on matters to be taken into account in determining questions relating to the definition of disability' is available on line at: www.drc.org.uk/law/codes.asp.

whether it can wait any longer for the employee to return to work or whether it should dismiss the employee.

In reaching that decision, the company will need to take into account all the relevant circumstances, including the length of the employee's absence from work and the organisational and financial impact that the employee's absence is having on the business. If, for example, the employee has a chronic condition with an uncertain prognosis and the company is having difficulty covering for his or her absence, it may be reasonable to dismiss. On the other hand, if the employee has been absent for an extended period but the company has established satisfactory cover arrangements and the employee is likely to be fit to return in the near future, it is likely to be unreasonable to dismiss. The decision is a managerial, not a medical one.

■ Contractual ill health benefits

A company will normally be acting in breach of contract if it dismisses an employee on ill-health grounds before the employee's right to occupational sick pay has expired (unless the contract provides for this). That the employee has not yet exhausted his or her entitlement to sick pay is also a factor to be taken into account in considering the fairness of a dismissal (although it is not conclusive).

If the employee's terms and conditions include long-term disability benefits (a PHI scheme) the employer should always seek advice before dismissing the employee.

If an employee's health does not improve whilst he or she is on a rehabilitation programme, then this usually indicates that his or her condition is more serious than initially thought and this fact may help the employee's GP to obtain quicker NHS appointments for investigation and/or treatment. It also means there may be less speculation about whether an employee qualifies for long-term disability benefits such as an employer-run PHI scheme or for ill-health early retirement.

■ Ill-health early retirement

Depending on the rules of the company's occupational pension scheme, ill-health early retirement may be an alternative to dismissal on the grounds of capability. There are, though, three points to bear in mind in handling ill-health early retirements.

First, employees who 'retire' are not normally, in law, treated as 'dismissed' employees and so lose the right to claim unfair dismissal. However, there have been cases where employees have persuaded employment tribunals to treat them as having been dismissed where they have been able to establish that they had not truly consented to retire as an alternative to dismissal. Most of theses cases arise because the employer has not made it clear in writing what are all the terms of the retirement and the employee was expecting more generous terms (such as a voluntary severance payment) which might have been available had they been dismissed.

Second, if the employment tribunal does hold that an employee has been dismissed rather than retired, the tribunal would also, from 1 October 2004, hold that the employee had been automatically unfairly dismissed if the employer has not followed the statutory minimum discipline and dismissal procedure (see pages 27–31) before the retirement takes effect.

Third, employees who are in law treated as retired rather than dismissed nevertheless retain the right to claim they have been discriminated against under the DDA. The fact that an employee appeared to consent to the retirement may provide only limited protection for the employer against such a DDA claim.

To avoid these pitfalls we recommend that in cases where employees are retiring on the grounds of ill-health the employer:

- specifically explores whether there are any reasonable adjustments that could be made as an alternative to early retirement on ill-health grounds

- unless an exemption applies (see page 29) follows the formalities of the statutory discipline and dismissal procedure set out in summary on pages 27–31. This means ensuring that, before the retirement takes effect, the employer writes to the employee setting out the reasons why ill-health early retirement is being considered (including a summary of what was considered and rejected as possible adjustments under the DDA), holds a meeting with the employee to allow him or her to state his or her case, writes to the employee to explain the outcome of the meeting and offers the employee an appeal

- spells out in writing (one letter may cover this point and the one above) the terms of the pension and any other payments to be made well before the effective date of the retirement so as to give employees the chance to raise any errors or misunderstanding. The letter should expressly state that no other payment or benefits apply, and

- the employer should require the employee to sign acknowledging and agreeing to the terms and the date that the retirement starts.

● Employee who suffers a catastrophic illness

There may be cases where the employee suffers a catastrophic illness (such as a severe stroke or is diagnosed with untreatable lung cancer where death is very likely within six months). Employers must not however make assumptions about an employee's prognosis – again, they must take advice from an occupational health adviser and/or the employee's GP/specialist. A person who suffers a severe stroke, for example, may recover a significant amount of their functions within six months. There will be very few cases where no consultation is necessary for example because it would be futile.

If the employee is not able to participate in the consultation the employer should consult with the employee's representative, perhaps a spouse or other close relative, or trade union official.

In certain circumstances, and this may include a catastrophic illness, an employment contract can be terminated by operation of the legal principle known as frustration. The principle, and the difficulties of predicting where it applies, are considered on page 26.

Overcoming barriers to rehabilitation

In this section we look at some of the main barriers to successful rehabilitation and a more proactive approach to sickness absence management. The main barriers are:

- Poor access to occupational health advice

- Reluctant managers
- Medical certificates and the GP
- Reluctant employees
- NHS delays

Poor access to occupational health advice

Without a doubt, an employer that does not have access to occupational health advice will find it difficult to reap the benefits of rehabilitation. On pages 61–9 we consider, therefore, the possibilities for improving access.

Reluctant managers

● Reasons for reluctance

Managers may be reluctant to support rehabilitation initiatives for a number of reasons, most of which arise from faulty perception, namely that rehabilitation is:

- too much effort
- too complicated, and
- results in more DDA-protected employees on the company's headcount.

● Isn't rehabilitation too much effort?

Unless senior managers (and the personnel function if there is one) persuade line managers in particular that rehabilitation is worth it, a culture supportive of rehabilitation initiatives will not take root. Whilst it is probably true that a case management approach, which places responsibility on individual managers to be proactive, means more effort for those managers unfortunate enough to have an attendance problem, the company as a whole reaps the dividends. This is why a strategy for maximising attendance – with rehabilitation at its centre – must be led and reinforced by senior management. Unless it is, dismissal will often be raised as the first, not the last resort, with all that represents in terms of lost experience and skills, higher recruitment costs and exposure to expensive litigation and poor workforce morale.

▪ Isn't rehabilitation too complicated?

Most rehabilitation is not rocket science. Whilst really complicated medical conditions will require specialist occupational health input, the vast majority of long-term absences are due to relatively straightforward medical conditions that are amenable to rehabilitation. If a line manager or the employee feels that there are no temporary work modifications in the area, then it is worthwhile looking at the guidance on pages 86–90 (as well as the list of possible adjustments under disability discrimination legislation (see pages 21–22)) for extra ideas and checking if this is really the case. Asking the employee what work changes to make in order to facilitate a return to work can be enlightening and gains 'buy in' from the employee (see below on 'reluctant employees').

It is especially important when dealing with employees who qualify (or might do) for protection under the DDA to think broadly about rehabilitation and/or reasonable adjustments. Employment tribunals take a dim view of employers who put the onus on employees (and their GPs) to suggest possibilities when it is the employer who best knows its operating practices and working arrangements. It is also unwise, given the potential liabilities in a DDA case, to leave this assessment entirely to a line manager to consider without occupational health support.

▪ Doesn't rehabilitation just result in more DDA-protected employees on the company's headcount?

Managers often perceive that if they spend a long time trying to maintain an absent employee on the books or getting them back to work, the more likely that employee is to acquire protection under the DDA triggering the legal obligation to make reasonable adjustments and the possibility of a claim for unlimited compensation. To some employers this concern about 'opening the door' to a future DDA claim acts as a significant disincentive to consider rehabilitation measures before dismissal.

Making a decision to dismiss quickly rather than try rehabilitation measures does not protect the company from successful employment tribunal claims. Yes, it is correct that, normally, employees must suffer a qualifying injury or illness for at least a year before acquiring protection under the DDA. However it is not safer to dismiss an employee before that year is up because:

- the definition of a disability under the DDA is so complicated and wide that, particularly in relation to mental health disorders, dismissing an employee quickly does not guarantee the company avoids a DDA claim. By the time of dismissal, the employee may already have protection and a tribunal might, with the benefit of hindsight, consider that the employer knew enough to be on notice that the employee might have protection (see page 21)

- some employees may have had their condition for less than a year but they will be protected if it is likely to last for at least that amount of time

- there are some conditions that may become covered by the DDA even if they have not lasted 12 months (see page 17)

- employees are also protected under the DDA if the consequences of their illness or injury are masked by treatment (for example, an employee taking thyroxine tablets for hypothyroidism), unless they have been completely cured before the 12-month period from diagnosis expires (see page 17) and

- in any event, employees with at least one year's service will have unfair dismissal protection and, over the years, the standard expected of employers has been rising in terms of seeking alternatives (such as considering a phased return to work on a part-time basis) before deciding to dismiss (see pages 24–6).

It is important, therefore, that line managers receiving training or advice on the legal reasons why they should diligently consider rehabilitation measures.

Medical certificates and GPs

The issues

A GP's primary duty is to his or her patient. GPs will always act, when he or she feels that a choice has to be made, as the patient's advocate rather than as an objective assessor acting in the interests of all parties, including the employer. It is no surprise, therefore, that many employers have a negative view of GPs. There are a number of connected issues and beliefs:

- many employers (and employees) believe that an employee is beyond an employer's reach, including rehabilitation efforts, so long as they have a doctor's certificate stating they are unfit to work

- that there is a 'sick note culture' that contributes to an all or nothing attitude to sickness and working which runs counter to the spirit of rehabilitation

- that GPs can be easily manipulated by employees and are 'soft' when it comes to managing their patients' expectations for a medical certificate

- that GPs don't have the time to deal with individual cases to the degree necessary for a successful rehabilitation programme

- some GPs are suspicious of an employer's motives and are hostile to rehabilitation efforts

- that employees are signed off for longer than medically necessary

- some GPs are content to give only a vague diagnosis, and

- it can take an unreasonably long time to obtain medical reports from GPs.

It would be reasonable to say that all these factors may play a part in prolonging sickness absences and act as barriers to a successful rehabilitation programme. We consider some of these issues below.

The sick note culture

In many cases GP's decisions are crucial in determining an employee's fitness to work. Under the Department of Work and Pensions (DWP) 'healthy work and recovery' agenda, the Government is taking steps to persuade GPs to take a broader view of the long-term interests of patients and is encouraging them to provide positive and informed advice about work, recovery and rehabilitation. It has recently issued the following advice[11] to GPs regarding sickness absence:

'You should always bear in mind that a patient may not be well served in the longer term by medical advice to refrain from work, if more appropriate clinical management would allow them to stay in work or return to work'.

GPs are also being reminded by the DWP to bear in mind appropriate (and up to date) clinical guidelines. For example, in 1999 the Royal College of GPs issued clinical guidelines for the management of acute low back pain which explain that, generally speaking, the most appropriate clinical advice is to keep active and that, for many people, staying at work or returning to work as soon as possible, is beneficial[12].

Employers cannot, realistically speaking, stay one step ahead of doctors working to old-fashioned advice – but an occupational health adviser can. This is another good reason for involving occupational health support at a very early stage particularly where it appears that an employee has been signed off for a lengthy period without regard to the possibility of rehabilitation.

The DWP's advice also recognises that some GPs do find it hard to refuse certificates to employees who are expecting them.

At the time of writing we understand that consideration is being given by the NHS for pilot projects under which responsibility for certificates is transferred from GPs to occupational health professionals. Associations will keep employers informed of any developments in due course.

In the meantime, the DWP's initiatives open up the possibility for more partnership between employers and GPs to break down the sick note culture. For example, employers can:

---

11 IB204 – a guide for registered medical practitioners, available from www.dwp.gov.uk/medical

12 'Clinical Guidelines for the Management of Acute Low Back Pain', Royal College of General Practitioners, Feb 1999, available online: www.rcgp.org.uk/press/1999/9001.asp

- Raise the awareness of GPs in their area; write and inform them of their rehabilitation policy and methods of supporting employees returning to work. GPs do tend to remember the businesses that are willing to offer rehabilitation. The result is that some GPs will ask the employee what work modification(s) their manager can provide to allow a return to work if they receive such letters.

- Refer to the DWP's advice (see above) when corresponding with GPs on individual cases.

Breaking down this culture is a long-term objective and not entirely in an employer's control. Also, there may be good clinical reasons why a GP continues to sign off a particular employee even though a business has offered some temporary work modifications to facilitate a return to work. If, though, a business feels that the GP is being unreasonable, they have made the GP aware of what they can offer and the GP is continuing to sign off the employee, the employer can only make headway by seeking the advice of an occupational physician (but not an occupational nurse) whose advice can be used to challenge the GP's stance. We also suggest the company seek advice from EEF Associations where there are conflicts over medical evidence (see pages 99–100).

GPs signing employees off for longer than is medically necessary

There is evidence that, generally speaking, employees are signed off for longer than is medically necessary for a number of conditions, although the reasons for it are complex. The DWP has given GPs up-to-date evidence-based medical guidance to consider when certifying people off work.

The DWP's advice to GPs sets out indicative recovery periods for common operations (hernia, hysterectomy, etc). For example, a straightforward hernia operation needs 2 to 3 weeks at the most for full recovery, however most GPs will sign off an individual for around 6 weeks.

Similarly, the evidence suggests that a woman who has had a hysterectomy needs 7 weeks (even less, depending on the medical procedure used) to recover fully, although employees are normally still signed off for 3 months.

If, though, the GP signs an employee off for the conventional recovery period it is not surprising that employees may feel justified in staying off work for that duration and only the highly motivated might return to work sooner.

The guidance from the DWP is readily available[13] and the indicative recovery times for the commonest operations and for heart problems are tabled overleaf. It assumes that the patient has made an uneventful recovery with no significant complications such as wound infection.

Post-operative time (in weeks) to full activity including work

Operation	Laparoscopic	Open	
Abdominal/groin hernia	1–2	2–3	
Appendectomy	1–2	2–3	
Cholecystectomy	2–3	3–5	
Hysterectomy	Lap. assisted vaginal	Abdominal	
	3	7	
Return to work after	Angioplasty	Infarction*	CABG**
cardiac illness	0–4	4–6	4–8

* Heart attack   **Coronary Artery Bypass Graft

(Source: British Heart Foundation)

It will take time for this advice to change GP's custom and practice in this area of medicine and for GPs and their patients to accept that recovery from operations is a lot quicker than 10 or 20 years ago. However, knowledge of these trends may make an employer feel on stronger grounds to write to the GP about such cases, along the following lines:

'Dear Dr.

We understand from advice issued to GPs by the DWP that a hernia operation/appendectomy/cholecystectomy/hysterectomy usually takes X weeks to recover and to get back to full activity including work. If there are no significant clinical complications, we would be happy to provide temporary work modifications to facilitate an earlier return to

---

13 See the DWP website: www.dwp.gov.uk/medical/hot.asp#return

work than that stated on the current medical certificate. We can offer [set out the proposed rehabilitation options such as: part time work/ provide transport/other typical rehabilitation measures].'

The employer will require the employee's consent to write such a letter to the GP if seeking a response about an individual employee. Alternatively, the employer could just send the letter to the GP as a way of highlighting the issue, whilst recognising that, unless the employee has given consent, the GP is not obliged to respond. The GP will, though, be aware that the employer knows about the Desk Aid and may think about a medical certificate for a shorter duration for the next employee from that business.

Vague medical certificates

If a GP gives a vague diagnosis, what can an employer do?

The Government's guide to GPs on medical certificates[14] emphasises that a medical certificate should contain an accurate diagnosis of the patient's disorder which has led to the GP advising the patient to refrain from work.

It is quite common, though, for employers to receive medical certificates which do not give a diagnosis but cite vague symptoms such as TATT ('tired all the time'), 'debility', 'fatigue', 'exhaustion' or 'malaise'. Some of the main practical issues about such medical certificates are considered below.

Referral to an occupational health adviser

It is not common for GPs to sign employees off sick for lengthy periods without specifying a diagnosis. However, if the employer does receive a vague medical certificate for a period of two weeks or more (or a succession of them) then the employer should consider a referral to an occupational health adviser who, in turn, can prompt the GP to give a further explanation and/or consider further medical investigation. Even if a clearer diagnosis is not forthcoming, the employer should still seek views on possible rehabilitation measures (see pages 93–8).

---

14 IB 204 issued by the Department for Work and Pensions is available online at: www. dwp.gov.uk/medical/medicalib204/index.asp

Can we withhold sick pay if we receive a vague medical certificate?

The employer is only entitled to withhold SSP (or company sick pay) if it has good reason to dispute eligibility. These types of pay are considered separately below.

SSP

To qualify for SSP the employer has to be satisfied that the employee is incapable, because of a specific disease or disablement, of doing work that can reasonably be expected to be done under the contract of employment. TATT, fatigue, etc, whilst not diagnoses of a specific condition are symptoms that are 'disabling' the employee. Strictly speaking, an employer would not be able to dispute entitlement to SSP for this reason. The employer could dispute it, though, if the doctor had written only 'unfit for work' or had left blank that part of the medical certificate (or the employer had other reasonable grounds for disputing eligibility).

Government assistance for establishing entitlement to SSP

If the employer is concerned about whether an employee is entitled to be paid SSP, it can ask the Inland Revenue (which oversees the administration of SSP) to arrange for an opinion from their Medical Services Officers. The employer can ask for an opinion when:

- the employer disputes whether the illness is genuine

- the employee is off sick for longer than a defined period for a particular type of illness. These so-called 'control periods' for common illnesses are listed in the Inland Revenue SSP Manual[15]. For example, for 'headaches and migraines', the period is one month. It is also a month for 'debility,' and other illnesses not yet diagnosed. After the specified period has expired, the employer can seek an opinion on the employee's eligibility for SSP, or

---

15 See Inland Revenue publication CA 30 'SSP Manual for Employers' and chapter entitled 'Control of sick absence', www.inlandrevenue.gov.uk/pdfs/emp2003/ca30_03.pdf

- the employee has had frequent short periods of absence and submits either self-certificates or medical certificates. The help of Medical Services may be available where the employee has been sick for four or more short periods in a 12-month period. The report will indicate whether there are reasonable grounds for the employee having frequent absences from work for medical reasons which information the employer can use to help it decide whether or not it should pay SSP on the next occasion that the employee is sick.

Full details of how to apply for such medical reports are available from www.inlandrevenue.gov.uk/pdfs/emp2003/ca30_03.pdf

Company sick pay

In our view there are significant risks attached to withholding company sick pay on the grounds that an employee has submitted one or more vague medical certificates. There are a number of reasons for this which are considered below.

What does the contract of employment say?

First, whether or not the employer is entitled to withhold company sick pay if it receives a vague medical certificate will turn on the terms of the company sick pay scheme. Most schemes simply require the employee to produce a medical certificate after the 8th day of absence and do not lay down any further requirements. If the employer wishes to pay sick pay only if the employee submits a medical certificate citing a specific diagnosis then, in our view, the contract must expressly state that.

Second, the employer must have a good reason to dispute whether the employee is entitled to the sick pay. It does not necessarily follow that because a medical certificate is vague that the employee is not genuinely ill. It will be incumbent on the employer to seek further advice to establish whether the employee is eligible for sick pay or risk being in breach of contract.

Even if company sick pay is payable only at the company's discretion, the employer would still be expected to take steps to establish what the medical position is, otherwise it could be held to be in breach of contract in the way that it exercises its discretion. Again, if the employer wishes to withhold sick pay in circumstances where sick pay is discretionary and the employee has not submitted a medical certificate specifying a clear diagnosis, then it should expressly state that submission of a vague medical certificate may be one of the grounds for exercising its discretion not to pay. This would require careful drafting and employers should seek specific advice from their EEF Association.

The need to take advice before taking any action

As to the risks of withholding company sick pay, if the employer fails to pay it without good reason, the employer is very likely to be acting in breach of contract. Non-payment of company sick pay is normally sufficiently serious to amount to a constructive dismissal (which may be unfair). Alternatively, the employee could bring a claim of breach of contract and/or unlawful deduction from wages.

Also, withholding sick pay is 'action short of dismissal' for the purposes of the statutory discipline and dismissal procedure and so employers will be required to follow the mandatory procedural rules (when they come into force from 1 October 2004) before stopping the pay (see pages 27–31). In summary, this means writing to the employee explaining the reason why the employer is proposing to withhold the pay, holding a meeting with the employee, writing to explain the outcome and offering an appeal (see pages 27–31).

In practice, the fact that the employer has withheld sick pay may influence a tribunal considering at the same time any other claim the employee may bring, such as unfair dismissal or a breach of the DDA. We suggest, therefore, employers seek advice from their EEF Association before withholding company sick pay for any reason, including on the grounds that the employee has submitted a vague medical certificate.

Dealing with reluctant employees

■ The issues

Practically speaking, it is rare for an employee who has exhausted company sick pay to refuse to try a rehabilitation programme (although it is more likely if the employee has a personal injury claim pending, especially one against the employer for a workplace illness or injury (see page 129)).

However, where the employee has not exhausted sick pay, he or she may be faced with the choice of co-operating with an employer's rehabilitation efforts (for example, a phased return to work) after, say 8 weeks' absence, or staying off work on full sick pay for 12 weeks. Some employees would naturally opt for the latter. An employee's motivation can, therefore, be very important to the success of rehabilitation initiatives particularly for employers with generous company sick pay schemes and/or long-term disability benefits (such as PHI). This is just one of the factors that is leading some companies to review PHI arrangements.

What can be done about it? If an employee appears not to be co-operating, the employer's options turn on the facts of each case and the terms of an employee's contract of employment. We consider some of the issues below on pages 123–9.

■ Ask occupational health adviser to contact GP

The first step for an employer that suspects an employee is reluctant to consider rehabilitation is to raise this with the company's occupational health adviser. If the occupational health advice is that the employee is fit to return to work with temporary modifications, then the employer should talk to the employee, listen to his or her concerns and offer reassurance that a return to work is in everybody's best interest. Good occupational health professionals will also have spent some time during their consultation trying to convince the employee that no harm will come from the rehabilitation programme and explaining that the employee will be carefully and regularly monitored and medical concerns addressed if they arise.

The most likely reason for the employee's reluctance is the fact that the employee is holding a GP's medical certificate signing the employee off for a particular duration, say, 3 months. The GP plays a vital role in persuading the employee that this does not necessarily mean that the employee must refrain from doing any work at all during this period. It is very useful in such situations for the occupational health professional to write to the employee's GP explaining the clinical reasons for their opinion and the proposed rehabilitation programme and inviting the GP to raise any significant clinical reason why the employee should not start it. In such situations, GPs rarely raise any significant concerns and, in fact, may welcome an occupational health adviser taking off them the responsibility for persuading the employee that returning to work is in their best interests. This allows the GP to stay on good terms with their patient.

The involvement of an occupational health adviser may be enough to bring the employee round. If it is not, consider the issues below.

▪ Can we withhold sick pay if the employee refuses to co-operate with a rehabilitation programme?

What is the position if an employee continues to refuse to co-operate with a suggested rehabilitation programme to which their GP or specialist has no significant clinical objection?

SSP

We deal with the circumstances in which an employer can withhold SSP for a reason relating to the employee's incapacity on pages 120–21.

Company sick pay

What does the contract of employment say?

It would be preferable if company sick pay schemes expressly provided that continuing eligibility for sick pay depended on the employee's reasonable co-operation with the company's arrangements for managing the absence, including co-operation with measures for rehabilitation and obtaining medical advice. However, it is likely that few sick pay schemes contain such detailed provisions.

In the absence of such provisions, deciding what are the employer's rights in relation to company sick pay is not a straightforward matter. Much will depend on the nature of the proposed rehabilitation and the interaction with the terms of the employee's contract of employment and the company sick pay scheme.

Conflicting views on the employer's rights

Take, for example, an employee who works full-time as a production operative but is signed off sick with a lower back problem. The occupational health adviser has suggested the employee can continue to work full-time on adjusted duties and the GP has raised no significant clinical objections to the proposed rehabilitation programme.

It is arguable that the request for the employee to come to work on adjusted duties would be a lawful and reasonable instruction, i.e. requiring the employee to work within his or her competence and would not be in breach of the implied duty of trust and confidence. (It might be a breach if, for example, the company were to ask its financial controller to work on reception.) Some contracts of employment expressly give employers the right to require an employee to work flexibly, however, it is arguable that it is not necessary to have an express clause if all the employer is asking of the employee is that he or she performs part of their duties in accordance with a rehabilitation programme.

On the other hand, it is also arguable that, as long as the employee has a medical certificate and has complied with any other qualifying criteria for company sick pay, they are excused further attendance and the employer would be in breach of contract to withhold sick pay. But the purpose of rehabilitation initiatives is to open up a dialogue with the GP and the employee, in effect, to modify the medical certificate and obtaining the GP's agreement that the employee is fit for some work. If the GP agrees that the employee is fit enough to perform the amended duties then arguably an employee who is still unco-operative without good reason is not entitled to company sick pay.

The position may be further complicated if the proposed rehabilitation programme may result in the employee being worse off financially than staying off work and claiming sick pay. Suppose in the above example the occupational adviser had recommended that the employee return to work initially on a part-time basis, even though he or she has not yet exhausted company sick pay. There is an argument that, by definition, the period when the employee is not working he or she is sick and should, therefore, still be entitled to receive company sick pay for those hours. This would mean that an employer who did not pay sick pay for at least those hours would be acting in breach of contract.

The need to take advice before taking any action

In our view, there is no clear cut answer to the question of whether an employer can withhold sick pay only on the grounds that the employee will not try a rehabilitation programme (as opposed to failing to comply with other aspects of an employer's absence management procedure such as complying with the notification rules).

In practice, most employers do take steps to protect the employee's financial position (see pages 127–9) which removes the biggest disincentive to trying out a rehabilitation programme and which achieves the employer's main aim, which is to have the employee return to productive work as soon as possible.

If despite assurances that pay will be protected during a rehabilitation programme (or where pay is not the issue) the employee still refuses to co-operate, then companies should seek specific advice before withholding sick pay. There are a number of reasons for this.

First, withholding sick pay is 'action short of dismissal' for the purposes of the statutory discipline and dismissal procedure and so employers will be required to follow the mandatory procedural rules (when they come into force from 1 October 2004) before stopping the pay (see pages 27–31).

Second, the employer risks being found to be in breach of contract for wrongfully withholding sick pay if it has not fully consulted the employee and made significant efforts to understand the medical position and iron out any conflicts. The burden is a tough one. Further, if the employer makes the wrong decision and is held to be in breach of contract then this may influence the employment tribunal considering either a related unfair dismissal and/or a DDA claim in the event the employee leaves and brings proceedings.

■ Can we dismiss a reluctant employee?

On balance, a tribunal is likely to find fair the dismissal of an employee where the medical evidence suggests that the employee is capable of doing some work but the employee is being unreasonably unco-operative. However, it is likely to be unfair (and a breach of contract unless the contract provides otherwise) to dismiss before the employee has exhausted his or her entitlement to company sick pay. The employee's conduct is also a matter to be taken into account by tribunals in considering whether an employer has met its duty to make reasonable adjustments under the DDA.

However, given the near certainty of a claim of unfair dismissal and possibly disability discrimination, we strongly advise employers to seek advice from their EEF Association before dismissing in these circumstances.

What if there is a conflict of opinion between the occupational health adviser and the GP about the scope for rehabilitation?

The first step is for the employer to ask the occupational health adviser to try and resolve the conflict with the GP, or at least to narrow down the area of conflict.

After considering the GP's view, the occupational health adviser may stick to his or her original advice, that rehabilitation is an appropriate option. In deciding what to do next in managing the employee's absence, the employer is entitled to choose which advice to rely on. However, the employer must be satisfied that the occupational health adviser has taken into account any points raised by the GP. The issues raised above on pages 99–100 again become relevant.

Pay and job protection

A recent survey of employers' approaches to rehabilitation conducted by the workplace research organisation IRS[16] found that nearly 80 % of employers who responded included some form of job and/or income protection when implementing rehabilitation. Clearly, employees are going to be more willing to co-operate with rehabilitation initiatives if they do not lose out financially or lose their connection with their original job. Options employers typically considered include:

- maintaining sick pay even though an employee is returning to work on a phased basis

---

16 'Rehabilitation at work' in IRS Occupational Health Review, Sept/Oct 2002

- paying the employee's normal pay (minus, for example, any shift premium if shifts not worked)

- guaranteeing that the employee will be treated as holding his or her substantive role for a specified period, say, six months, after the employee returns to work to adjusted duties or an alternative job

- if the employee is permanently re-deployed to another, less well paid role, offering some degree of personal pay protection for a reasonable period, say a year, or freezing the employee's pay until the rate for the new job catches up with it (but see pages 101–102)

- where employers offer a flexitime system, allowing employees to build up debit time for the normal working hours not worked, to be cleared over an agreed period

    There are pitfalls with this approach: if employees have to work very long hours to clear a backlog of debit time this can cause ill-health problems or trigger a recurrence of the original condition (particularly relevant for mental health disorders).

- using up annual leave for the period of rehabilitation. For example, where an employee returns to work for a period of two weeks on half days only, using annual leave to cover the half days not worked. In our view, this is likely to be counter-productive for reasons similar to those indicated above for flexitime. It could also be interpreted as employers requiring employees to use annual leave in respect of those parts of the working week where they are covered by a medical certificate. Arguably, it is a breach of the Working Time Regulations. However, employers may continue to do this in respect of contractual holiday in excess of the WTR allowance.

- special paid leave: involves creating a new category of paid leave, separate to sick pay, to cover rehabilitation.

What the company is prepared to offer depends, of course, on how generous the employer's sick benefits are, that is, how much employees perceive they are 'giving up' by coming back to work earlier than they otherwise would.

Remember too that, if the employee has a qualifying disability, the employer may need to make a reasonable adjustment to its arrangements for certain terms and conditions so as not to disadvantage the employee (for example in the operation of an attendance bonus scheme). Companies are advised to seek detailed advice from their EEF Association on this topic.

▪ Employees with work-related personal injury claims

Employees may be particularly reluctant to co-operate with rehabilitation measures if they have personal injury claims pending against their employer for work-related injuries or illnesses. Employers too may be inhibited in exploring rehabilitation believing it may have a negative impact on their defence of the claim.

We suggest employers proactively discuss rehabilitation with their insurers as soon as they become aware of a claim or possible claim. Employees with PI claims should, in principle, be treated no differently to other ill or injured employees and so employers should explain the possibilities for rehabilitation set out in this section. This would be in keeping with the Association of Personal Injury Lawyers' Code of Practice on rehabilitation which is supported by all the main associations for insurers and personal injury lawyers in the UK.

The Code aims to promote the use of rehabilitation to ensure that the injured person makes the best and quickest possible medical, social and psychological recovery and to ensure that this aim is treated as importantly as the payment of compensation. To that end, solicitors acting for both the claimant and the insurer are under a duty to consider, at the earliest opportunity, whether rehabilitation would improve the injured person's long-term well-being. The Rehabilitation Code is available on line at www.apil.com/pdf/publicdocs/RehabRevisedApr03.pdf

Bearing in mind the claimant's solicitor's duty under the Code, if the company's occupational health adviser supports a rehabilitation programme and the employee is not co-operating, then the employer should raise it with the solicitors appointed by the company's insurers to defend the employee's claim. Even if the employer is found to be liable, employees who unreasonably fail to co-operate with rehabilitation initiatives (that is unreasonably fail to mitigate their financial loss) may suffer a reduction in any compensation due to them.

NHS delays

The length of NHS waiting lists for investigations and medical treatment is a significant factor in the length of time that people are signed off work and whether rehabilitation to work may be successful. This raises the question whether employers should pay for private treatment. This is considered on pages 90–93 along with the tax implications.

Integrating rehabilitation into existing arrangements for managing long-term ill-health

- **Does a greater focus on rehabilitation mean we should abandon our existing policy for handling long-term absence?**

It all depends. If the existing policy is inflexible and, if followed strictly, would not enable rehabilitation to be considered at an early stage, then the policy should be changed. For example, if a home visit or consultation is not triggered until the employee is absent for many weeks or, say, until full sick pay has expired, the employer may miss the boat for effective rehabilitation.

Some long-tem absence policies provide that rehabilitation will be considered, along with redeployment, as an alternative to dismissal if the employee is not able to return to work. The implication is that rehabilitation is a last ditch option. Policies like this need to be modernised, not only to reap the benefits of a rehabilitation approach but also to catch up with the ongoing requirement under disability discrimination legislation to make reasonable adjustments (see pages 20–24).

- **Can we unilaterally change our existing procedure for managing attendance?**

In many cases a company can decide unilaterally to change the process for managing attendance and its arrangements for dealing with long-term sickness absence (as opposed to the employee's benefits connected with sickness absence) just as it can, for example, when setting disciplinary rules. There is, though, a legal obligation to inform employees of certain changes which might flow from such a change (see pages 58–9). In any event, though, we strongly advise that all employees are involved in and informed of any changes before they are implemented (see pages 56–60).

Different considerations apply where the employer's existing policy or procedure:

- forms part of the employees' contract of employment and is so detailed that it specifies inflexible deadlines for certain steps (such as a referral to the company doctor or the line manager's first home visit) although in the private sector such detailed policies are rare, or

- where the existing procedure is not contractual but nevertheless its terms have been agreed collectively either with a trade union or employee representatives. A company may meet resistance in moving to the more flexible arrangements recommended in this Guide if the employees and/or their representatives wrongly interpret the company's approach as an attempt to cut back on the employees' existing rights.

Companies in this position should seek the advice of their employee relations adviser at their EEF Association.

● Wouldn't the unions see a focus on rehabilitation as a means of cutting down on sick pay entitlement?

There is growing recognition that rehabilitation measures are often in the best long-term interests of employees and the TUC is actively seeking to promote its benefits too. Trade unions will also support measures that reduce unnecessary sickness absence which in many workplaces places a strain on other colleagues. It is vital, however, that trade unions and other employee representatives are kept involved and informed about both the reason for introducing new initiatives as well as how it will be done (see pages 56–60) to avoid suspicion about the employer's motives.

Checklist for an effective attendance management policy emphasising rehabilitation

An effective attendance management policy and/or set of guidelines for managers should contain:

- guidance to managers to help them meet the following objectives:
  - maintain contact with the employee
  - within the employer's means, offer welfare support
  - adopt a case management approach (see pages 75–80)
  - as early as possible (that is, for example, not waiting until sick pay has expired) obtain medical evidence (preferably from an occupational health professional) on diagnosis, prognosis and suitability for rehabilitation, restricted duties and redeployment and to gauge the likely length of the absence and plan for covering it
  - consult the employee about medical information received
- a statement that rehabilitation initiatives apply as much to the treatment of employees who are still at work but have a chronic illness such as diabetes or asthma. Rehabilitation measures can significantly enhance their performance and productivity
- guidelines to ensure consistency of treatment. This would include specifying 'fallback' trigger periods for action such as when an individual should be referred to occupational health support, that is a 'no later than' date (see page 75), and the criteria against which the company will decide whether or not to pay for private treatment or investigations for an individual to aid a return to work (see page 92)
- the protocol for making contact with occupational health support (this should be via the personnel function or, where there is not one, a specified manager who has received relevant training which EEF can provide (see pages 37–8))
- a checklist of the information that should be included in instructions for a referral to occupational health support
- a checklist of possible rehabilitation measures/reasonable adjustments under the DDA for easy reference, and

- guidelines for triggering action against individual employees with an unacceptable level of attendance (see below).

In terms of guidance to individual employees, an effective attendance management policy should contain details on the:

- notification procedure: who to contact when absent because of illness and how

- qualification conditions for sick pay, both SSP and company sick pay (highlighting differences, if any, for the latter) including rules about certifying sickness absence

- the role of various departments or individuals in managing attendance

- a statement on the employer's intention to consider rehabilitation measures in appropriate cases to enable employees to return to work and its commitment to maintaining contact with employees if they are absent on long term sick leave

- an obligation on the employee to co-operate with the employer's attendance management policy including keeping in touch during long-term absence and agreeing to provide medical reports

- if they exist (and we recommend they should (see pages 153–6)) the trigger levels for action on unacceptable levels of attendance. The policy should make it clear when formal steps will be taken to ensure that managers take a consistent approach, and

- a statement on the consequences of having a poor attendance record (see page 149). Employees must be made aware if levels of absence have certain consequences, such as triggering a particular stage of the attendance management procedure or disciplinary procedure. It should state that a poor attendance record may, ultimately, lead to dismissal.

We recommend that employers ensure that any policy expressly states that it does not form part of the contract of employment so that it is easier for the employer to revise the policy. If, however, an existing policy already forms part of employee's contractual terms and conditions, the employer will not be able to unilaterally alter its status (or, indeed, change its terms) without seeking agreement to the variation in the usual way (see Chapter 5.1, 'Changing contracts of employment' in the 2003/04 EEF Employment Guide, www.employmentguide.org.uk).

CASE STUDIES

|||||||||||||||||||||||||||||||||||||||||||||||||||||||||||||||||||||||||||||||||||||||||||||||||||||||||||||||||||||||||||

Case study 2 – managing an employee with lower back pain

Scenario 1

Fred is a 50 year old fettler who has had recurrent bouts of lower back pain for many years and is off sick awaiting physiotherapy to help with the pain. He has good days and bad days with respect to the pain.

Action

His manager has maintained weekly contact and encouraged him to come into work for a chat after a few weeks of absence, which he has done. This has allowed him to keep in contact with his co-workers, catch up with what is happening in the workplace and the business and stay in the lottery syndicate!

Scenario 2

The occupational health nurse who comes once a week sees Fred at the manager's request and points out that it might be beneficial to pay for physiotherapy privately as the NHS waiting list in the area, for physio, is eight weeks.

Action

Maintaining contact and paying for physio has probably helped in Fred's willingness to do some part-time work (four hours a day) soon after he starts his physiotherapy. He finds sitting for too long or standing for too long a problem and normally has an hour's car journey to get into work (because of traffic) and a further 15 minutes finding a parking slot and walking to his workplace from the car park. It is, therefore, agreed that, for a month, he starts after the morning rush and finishes before the afternoon traffic worsens and is allowed to park in a reserved slot near his department. Fred normally works a rotating three shifts system but as he is being reviewed weekly by the occupational health nurse and seeing a physio, the manager agrees to let him stay on days for a while, to be reviewed in a month.

Scenario 3

The fettlers have to carry trays of product on a trolley to their own work area from the central stores.

Action

The manager has talked to the employees in the section and they have agreed to take it in turns to bring Fred his trays. The business has sought occupational health advice and the manager reviews the job and work area with Fred and the occupational health nurse. It is clear that the wooden stool that Fred sits on will cause him to stoop too much and a height adjustable chair with a back rest is found in one of the offices for him to use.

Outcome

Fred has six sessions of physio and has been taught by the physio how to improve his posture. Over a period of four weeks Fred builds up his hours to full-time work and soon after returns to shift working. The assessment of Fred's job identified that a lot of the employees were having manual handling problems with the trolley for carrying trays of product and a scissors platform trolley was ordered that would stop them having to stoop to lift the heavy trays. The occupational health nurse had obtained free leaflets on 'Back pain at work: a guide for people at work and their employers' that she distributed to all the employees and managers in the business to raise awareness of the things that both employees and managers could do to reduce back problems (details of availability are online: www.facoccmed.ac.uk/Content/pubs_list.htm#backs). The information made it clear to everyone that you did not have to be pain free to return to work and that, in many cases, taking time off work won't help and inactivity could make the problem worse.

||||||||||||||||||||||||||||||||||||||||||||||||||||||||||||||||||||||||||||||||||||||||||||||||||||||||

Case study 3 – managing an employee with stress

Scenario 1

A medical certificate with 'stress', for two weeks duration, arrives in payroll for a 35 year old female clerical worker.

Questions

As the medical certificate was posted the previous week, did the line manager know the employee was not at work? Did the employee (or a representative) ring into work on the first day of her absence? Have the sickness absence notification procedures been complied with?

Comment

Stress, more than most reasons for sickness absence, needs good cooperation and communication between the line managers, the personnel function and occupational health advisers. A medical certificate for 'stress' needs more rapid intervention than a medical certificate for a 'fractured leg' because of the risk of the absence becoming very long-term and the even greater risk than normal of the employee losing confidence and motivation.

Actions

What – a telephone call to the employee; visiting at this stage may be too intrusive and unnecessary if she returns to work after the two weeks.

How – a quiet private area with the potential to be undisturbed for about half an hour. Whilst tactful enquiries amongst co-workers might give useful background information and highlight any problems in or outside work prior to the absence the employer also has a duty to keep the employee's medical information confidential from colleagues. In our view it may be better to ask the employee directly if there are any other relevant background issues.

When – preferably within the first few days of the absence but certainly before the medical certificate runs out. If a phone number is not available then an informal letter, although not ideal, will have to suffice. The objective is to begin a dialogue.

Why – this first contact is to give reassurance to the employee and show that you/the business care; this should be the tone of the ensuing conversation. There is often little value, at this stage, in asking 'when are you coming back to work' because it comes across as uncaring and because it has little bearing on how she will feel in two weeks time. It is best to use phrases like 'is there anything we can do to help', 'is there anything you need', 'we miss you' (or words to that effect), 'don't worry about things at work', 'get yourself better' und 'I will ring you on x date' i.e. just before the medical certificate is due to expire. Fixing a date to speak again is an important part of being proactive and keeping control of the situation. It is worth noting that the employee with a 'nervous breakdown' (medically, an acute stress reaction) will usually need about 10–14 days of rest and sleep before they can think reasonably clearly hence the reason for waiting two weeks before the next contact.

Who – ideally the person who contacts the employee should be the one who knows her the best; usually this is the line manager. In certain circumstances (see below) it may be sensible for the personnel officer or the occupational health adviser to be the prime contact but keeping the line manager fully informed. If the line manager has not dealt with a similar situation before, he or she will need help and support in deciding what to say, how to say it and what information to obtain (see pages 37–8).

Difficult situations

'She is too ill to talk herself/she doesn't want to talk' – have the above conversation with her partner or relative and aim to talk with her the next time you ring.

'The manager/supervisor is the cause of her problems' – this is difficult and needs tactful handling; there may be an underlying or aggravating reason for the absence such as bullying or harassment. Alternatively, there may be little substance to the allegation and, furthermore, the manager could become quite stressed and hurt.

Another manager should liaise with the employee (such as the personnel officer, occupational health adviser or a different/senior manger) but it is essential that any grievances are dealt with properly. It is unwise to wait and deal with it only if the employee tries to return to work. You should ask the employee if she feels well enough to send in a written note setting out her grievance. Bring to her attention the requirement under the statutory grievance procedure to put grievances in writing (from 1 October 2004). If she says she is not yet well enough, offer to meet her and a companion (see page 31 on the right to be accompanied) to start the process of investigating it further. Whilst it is necessary to investigate the grievance properly this needs to be balanced against not pressing the employee to deal too quickly with it if it would be detrimental to their health to do so. This is a complex situation and you should contact your EEF Association and your occupational health adviser for further advice.

Scenario 2

After two weeks a further medical certificate for stress is received, this time for four weeks' duration. Comment: the absence is now clearly heading towards long-term sickness.

Actions

What – regular (about once a month) meetings or case conferences are a good way of managing long-term sickness absence cases as well as monitoring employees who have returned to work and are on rehabilitation programmes. In this scenario, the employee will have been off work for about three weeks but with already the potential to be off for six weeks. The action plan should concentrate on maintaining contact with her by a further phone call (similar conversation topics as before and, if she is willing to talk about it, what has the GP advised and is she waiting for any treatment/counselling). The phone call also allows the opportunity to introduce the first step in a rehabilitation programme i.e. simply visiting the workplace for 'a cup of tea' (if necessary, it is worth arranging transport). Encourage employees to do this but do not pressurise them.

Who – ideally, the line manager concerned, the personnel officer and the occupational health adviser and the employee's chosen companion or union representative (see pages 31 and 75–80) who can be very helpful in progressing a rehabilitation programme.

Difficult situations

'Work-related stress' – the employee may not be able to face the workplace so a neutral venue (or a home visit) is worthwhile pursuing.

'Severe illness' – the suggestions made above may not be appropriate for employees suffering from severe clinical depression or anxiety until they have had suitable and sufficient treatment from (usually) a psychiatrist but it is worth trying to maintain contact on a monthly basis.

In both situations the company should be maintaining contact with its occupational health advisers for guidance on maintaining contact with the employee.

Scenario 3

It is clear from the second conversation that the GP thinks 'it will be months before she gets better'.

Comment

Passively waiting for medical certificates to expire in the case of someone who does not need psychiatric treatment results in unnecessarily prolonged sickness absence and reduces the likelihood of a return to work (remember, after six months absence, there is only a 50 % chance of successfully returning to work).

Actions

What – identify work/workplace modifications that might allow a return to work.

Who – this is relatively easy if you have an occupational health adviser who could also see her and give a medical opinion of the situation. They would also know that the main functional problems with stress tend to be poor stamina, reduced ability to concentrate and difficulties with short-term memory and would be able to consider the generic workplace interventions on pages 93–9 in the context of her actual clerical role. Without occupational health input, but knowing what her job entailed, the line manager and the personnel officer could reasonably assess possible modifications. For example, part-time work avoiding rush hour travel (even if this was four hours every other day) or altering work content (not dealing with telephone calls).

How – explain to the employee that you would like to help her get back to normal work and so wish to refer her to occupational health for a view on what might be possible. Explain this would probably involve asking her GP for his or her view (see pages 93–9 for obtaining medical consent and what to write).

Difficult situations

'She will be paid part-time wages for part-time work' – rehabilitation is unlikely to get off the ground if she would make more money remaining off sick. Be prepared to match sick pay if less than the reduced salary for part-time work for a defined period whilst she is doing the reduced duties to facilitate a return to work. Agree to review the arrangements at the end of the defined period (see further pages 101–102 on pay and job protection arrangements).

'The GP will not allow a return to work' – if you have occupational health advice, they may agree or disagree with the GP's view. If they disagree, find out what work modification they advise (occupational health advice in such situations tends to be cautious and the employee is unlikely to be harmed by a rehabilitation programme proposed by an occupational health adviser). The employer can choose to take the advice of an occupational physician but not an occupational health nurse in preference to the view of a GP. It is sensible in such situations for the occupational physician to write to the GP explaining the reason for his or her advice and inviting the GP to raise any significant clinical objections.

'She is waiting for some treatment (say, counselling) which will take many months on the waiting list' – a business has to decide on a case by case whether to pay for treatment privately (see pages 90–93) but it must also ensure employees are treated equitably otherwise those who do not receive that benefit may raise grievances or make a discrimination/unfair dismissal complaint. We recommend employers draw up transparent guidelines against which to assess each case (see page 92).

Scenario 4

Her manager has talked with her on the phone and persuaded her to come in for a 'cup of tea'. It is clear that recent changes in the workplace and at home have caused her a problem. Previously, the clerks/secretaries in the office tended to do one particular task but in order to cover for holidays and absences, everyone is now required to do all the jobs including answer queries from customers. She had found this particularly difficult when dealing with angry customers (she is normally quite a timid person) and on the day before she went off sick, she had a row with a customer on the phone. From the home point of view, she has been finding it difficult to deal with her elderly, frail mother who lives alone and needs her to go in every morning to help her out.

Comment

From a medical point of view, it is always useful with stress cases to ask the question 'why now?' – why has the sickness absence started now and not a month ago? It can help to identify the key factors/stressors to help resolve the situation. For the employer, this may mean asking the employee if there are any work-related issues in the background or if there are any other issues which the employer may be able to help with.

Actions

Consider changing the pattern of work – allowing her to work flexitime for a defined period whilst she seeks help for her mother.

Change or reduce the tasks or work content – perhaps, after discussion with her colleagues, she can stop doing the phone and increase some other aspect although you must not reveal confidential medical information to them without her consent (see page 54).

Provide further training or information – arrange for her to be trained in dealing with angry callers and decide whether other employees need the same kind of training. The organisation 'MindOUT' for mental health concerns has recently produced very useful guidance (available at www.mindout.net) called 'A practical guide to managing and supporting mental health in the workplace' that has a section entitled 'Advice for employees'. She would have benefited from being sent or given that section had it been available at the time.

Outcome: the employee was given a letter by her manager to take to her GP that listed the above rehabilitation programme. The GP was willing to allow a return to work with these modifications. She was regularly reviewed (every week) and was back to her normal job after three months when her mother had moved into warden-aided accommodation. It turns out that the GP had written to social services to speed up the process with her mother citing the difficulties that the employer was facing with her sickness absence caused in part by the situation with the mother.

Case study 4 – how should we handle an employee who goes off sick during disciplinary proceedings?

The first step is to find out as quickly as possible whether the employee is fit enough to attend a disciplinary hearing, even if not fit for work.

The preferable course is to ask the employee to see a doctor appointed by the company, ideally, one with specialist knowledge of the particular condition referred to in the medical certificate. Valuable time may be lost approaching the employee's GP first although the occupational health physician is likely to want to write to the GP for information, for which the employer should ask the employee for consent (see page 93).

In seeking a report from the doctor, whether the employee's or the company's, the purpose is to establish:

- just how sick the employee is (for example, is he or she well enough to understand the allegations and what the disciplinary process entails as well as being capable of preparing his or her case), and

- when and in what circumstances the employee will be fit to attend the hearing if not currently fit. It may be, for example, that the employee could attend the disciplinary hearing if certain adjustments were made, such as to the location of the hearing or allowing the employee to take breaks as and when needed.

Companies should follow the advice on pages 93–8 for obtaining good quality medical reports which are focussed on the problem in hand.

If the employee is not currently fit to attend, the company will need to consider whether it can postpone the hearing until the employee is fit. In relation to the new statutory discipline and dismissal procedure (which comes into force from 1 October 2004), there is an exemption which means that the employer is not required to apply it where it is not practicable to commence it or comply with its provisions within a reasonable period.

It is not clear how tribunals will interpret this exemption but it is likely that relevant factors they will consider are the seriousness of the charges, the nature of the evidence, etc. Employers will also need to take advice on the prognosis before concluding that they would have to wait for an unreasonable period in order to complete the procedure. In many cases the employer will in any case be able at least to commence the procedure. Even if the exemption applies, the employer's other legal obligations still remain – for example, to handle a dismissal fairly and consider the duty to make reasonable adjustments under the DDA.

Until the legislation is well established companies would be wise to seek advice before relying on the exemption. In general, it will be advisable to postpone the hearing, though, where relevant, evidence should be gathered from witnesses while recollections are fresh. The employee should also be invited to supply in writing his or her own statement in relation to the charge.

Only if the doctor is unable to give a prognosis for recovery or the estimated delay is plainly excessive given the seriousness of the charge should the company consider going ahead with the disciplinary hearing in the employee's absence. The company should send the employee full details of the disciplinary charge and the evidence against him or her (in accordance with the statutory discipline and dismissal procedure) and the employee should be invited to comment in writing. It is advisable to ask the employee to nominate a fellow employee or trade union official to represent his or her interests at the hearing.

Tackle frequent short-term absence

Introduction

Short-term erratic absence is difficult to plan for and is very disruptive. It is a fact of business life, though, that employees will be ill from time to time, and some more often than others, for a variety of reasons. In this section we consider what measures employers can take to tackle any unnecessary short-term absenteeism.

This Guide is not intended to encourage employers to force sick or injured employees to come to work but rather to help employers eradicate unnecessary absence. It is also our experience that employee relations are enhanced if employers work on the assumption that all frequent short-term absences are caused by genuine illness but have in place a mechanism for establishing if there are any underlying reasons for them. In this section, we recommend employers use return to work interviews for all employees for this purpose (see pages 168–78).

Causes of short-term absence

In the vast majority of cases, employees will state minor illnesses, colds, flu, migraine, stomach bugs and the like, as the reason for their short-term absence. The vast majority of sickness absence is genuine. But, tellingly, in the CBI's survey of absence in 2002 (see pages 34–5 above), when asked to estimate how much of their employees' absence might not be genuine, 82% of employers believed that up to 30% of absence may not be genuine sickness absence. This reflected the results of a CIPD survey of HR Managers[17] who estimated that a significant amount of sickness absence was not the result of sickness but included absence caused by home and family responsibilities and other non-genuine sickness reasons.

So, if there is large-scale sickness absence not caused by sickness, what is the reason – and how can it be tackled? Not all of it will be wilful skiving warranting disciplinary action.

There may be many complex factors why people might call in sick citing general minor illness which might mask other issues to do with aspects of people's working conditions or home lives including:

- poor working conditions (particularly if the work is boring, repetitive and/or physically demanding)
- long working hours with a lot of overtime
- poor morale, training and supervision
- bullying or harassment problems
- work-related stress
- difficult domestic circumstances including problems with children, and
- a culture where employees see paid sick leave as an entitlement, that is a form of additional holiday.

Eradicating unnecessary short-term absence – what works and why?

To tackle successfully the problem of unnecessary short-term absence employers need:

1   a mechanism to find out what the reason for the absence is and for teasing out any underlying causes. We recommend the return to work interview for this, and

2   a commitment to tackle any reasons revealed which:

---

17 Employee absence – a survey of management policy and practice (report 13), CIPD, published May 2000. Tel. 020 8263 3434.

- are in the employer's control (such as work design, training, hostile working conditions such as unlawful harassment, bullying, etc)

- suggest management is not using effective techniques to monitor or control the absence (such as ineffective notification procedures)

- are connected to rights employees may have which are relevant to the reasons for the absence. For example, some employees may have the statutory right to request flexible working or the right to parental leave. For others, the right to time off for dependants may be relevant. Alternatively, the employer may have a duty to make reasonable adjustments if the employee has a qualifying disability (see pages 20–24)

- are amenable to rehabilitation, or

- it is otherwise within the employer's resources to assist the employee and so remove the need for absence.

Ultimately, what works for a particular company will be highly dependent on many factors: company history, culture, management style, age and gender profile of the workforce, as well as labour turnover, etc. Without a doubt, though, some techniques seem to be universally more effective than others. In this section we look at the pros and cons of some of the most widely used management tools for controlling unnecessary short-term sickness absence.

In addition, employers often report that the effectiveness of some tools differs between manual and non-manual employees. Whilst that may be the case, EEF's view is that, if a company wants to embed a culture of maximum attendance, the core features of formal action (see pages 148–9), rigorous notification procedures (see pages 164–8) and return to work interviews (see pages 168–78) should be applied to everyone in a company.

How soon can companies expect improvements?

As the case study on page 7 demonstrates a company can experience a marked improvement in short-term absence levels within a few months.

Paradoxically, though, some companies report that attendance levels actually appear to deteriorate initially. If this happens it is usually because those managers who tended to under-record absence, for example, those who did not require employees to observe notification procedures or complete self-certificates, begin to improve their record keeping. Some companies also find that they do, in fact, have more of an attendance problem amongst non-manual staff than they thought.

List of management tools considered in this Guide for tackling frequent short-term absence

We consider the following management tools for tackling frequent short-term absence:

- Formal action/disciplinary action (pages 148–64)

- Rigorous notification procedures (pages 164–8)

- Return to work interviews (pages 168–78)

- Spot checks at an employee's home (page 178)

- Pre-employment screening (pages 178–9)

- Controls in sick pay schemes (pages 179–82)

- Inducements (including attendance bonuses) (pages 183–4)

- Team competition and absence 'league tables' (page 184)

- Making attendance count in employment decisions (redundancy selection, promotion, etc) (pages 185–6)

- Flexible working (page 186)

- Employee health initiatives (pages 186–7)

Formal action/disciplinary action

Early intervention to tackle frequent short-term absence is usually very effective. Following an informal word or counselling from a line manager, an employee's attendance record usually improves.

If it does not then the company needs to take more formal action. This raises several questions:

- what the nature of the action should be

- when to intervene, that is, what level of absence should trigger more formal action

- whether all absences should be counted in deciding whether to take more formal action

- when should the employer seek medical advice, and

- what procedural formalities the employer should observe when taking formal action.

These issues are dealt with in more detail below.

What type of formal action?

- Should we treat poor attendance as a disciplinary issue?

Many employers treat unacceptable levels of absence, including frequent short-term absences for genuine illness covered by self-certificates or medical certificates, as a 'disciplinary' issue. Employees with an unacceptable attendance record receive warnings under their employer's disciplinary procedure, as with instances of misconduct.

EEF does not advocate this approach. Many employment tribunals consider it unacceptable that employees who are absent with sickness or injury are put through a disciplinary process when their behaviour cannot be characterised as wilful misconduct (although see page 153 if there is a belief that the employee has committed misconduct).

Where their illness is genuine, employees, too, may struggle to appreciate that their employer is taking disciplinary action because of their attendance record, rather than because the employer doubts the genuineness of the illness or injury. This confusion can create grievances and may contribute to a poor employee relations climate. Employees are also likely to be aggrieved if a prospective new employer is given a reference about them which states that they have a disciplinary record but this is in fact based on their attendance record.

In addition, employees who are disciplined or dismissed under a disciplinary procedure for attendance issues relating to a disability may successfully claim that they have been discriminated against under the DDA (see pages 16–20, 20–24 and 157–9).

Though it is undoubtedly the case that some employers find that treating unacceptable levels of absence as a disciplinary matter is effective, in our view the risk of a finding of unfair (and, possibly, constructive) dismissal and/or breach of the DDA is now unacceptably high.

Is there an alternative non-disciplinary approach?

There is an alternative approach which does not invite such a level of risk. Normally, it will be fair for a company to dismiss an employee with a history of intermittent, short-term sickness absences if it has followed a fair attendance management procedure. By this we mean that the employer has dismissed on the grounds of incapability or some other substantial reason ('SOSR') and has:

- consulted with the employee about his or her attendance record

- given him or her an opportunity to improve it

- cautioned the employee about the consequences if attendance does not return to an acceptable level

- followed the statutory disciplinary and dismissal procedure (see pages 27–31). In summary, this means writing to the employee explaining the reason why the employer is proposing to dismiss, holding a meeting with the employee to allow him or her an opportunity to state his or her case, writing to explain the outcome and offering an appeal (see pages 27–31), and

- taken all the relevant circumstances into account (see pages 155–6).

There is no express legal requirement that an employer follow a staged caution procedure but it is usual for employers to give employees more than one opportunity to improve before dismissal is reached. Indeed, many employers' attendance management procedures follow very closely the stages of their misconduct procedure.

In our view it is safer, and employees will perceive it to be fairer, if employers give their employees at least two formal opportunities to be cautioned that, unless there is a sustained improvement in their attendance level, they will be dismissed.

Whatever approach employers follow, though, it is vital that employees are made aware of the standards expected of them and the consequences of a poor attendance record. As with disciplinary action, it is wisest to have a formal written policy for dealing with attendance. Whatever type of procedure is used all employees should be made aware, in writing, of any company rules that treat certain types or levels of absence as matters which could lead to formal action (if disciplinary, it should say so) and dismissal.

Interrelationship between return to work interviews and formal action to manage those employees with a poor attendance record

A return to work interview is an effective management tool for establishing the facts about a particular spell of absence, revealing any underlying causes within the company's control and for discouraging casual absence. It is not of itself a type of formal action against an employee with an unacceptable level of attendance. It may, though, provide the opportunity for informal counselling of such an employee under the company's attendance management procedure but should not be the forum for taking more formal action. There are a number of reasons for this, as set out below.

Reasons to keep separate the return to work interview from meetings for formal action against poor attendees

- The return to work interview should be brief and informal, giving the employee an opportunity to explain why he or she has been away sick and for the employer to cover the other issues set out in the checklist on pages 174–5 below.

- The effectiveness of the interviews as a two-way channel for communication about the absence is undermined if employees perceive them negatively as a forum for receiving some form of penalty. This applies whether or not the company deals with attendance issues under the disciplinary procedure or under a separate attendance management procedure (see pages 149–53).

- If the meeting is – or becomes part-way through – a disciplinary hearing, a meeting about the employee's capability to do the job, or a meeting in which the employee may receive formal action under an attendance management procedure, then the statutory right to be accompanied applies (see pages 163–4). That right does not apply to a fact-finding meeting such as a routine return to work interview just as it does not apply to a disciplinary investigation meeting. (A company's own formal procedure, though, may give employees wider rights, allowing them to be accompanied at investigation-type meetings and perhaps even a right to be 'represented' rather than accompanied).

- If during the return to work interview discrepancies arise or other factors emerge which lead the line manager to think that a disciplinary investigation is necessary, the line manager should stop the return to work interview and explain that he or she is considering implementing the disciplinary process. The same applies if the manager realises that a trigger under the attendance management procedure has been met (see pages 153–4).

- There may be circumstances where the new statutory discipline and dismissal procedure (see pages 27–31) which comes into effect from 1 October 2004, apply. For example, in certain cases, an employer must inform the employee in writing in advance of a meeting where action is to be taken of the reasons why the action is being proposed. Failure to follow any of the statutory procedural rules can result in a finding of automatic unfair dismissal and/or increased compensation (see page 30). Again, these procedural rules do not apply to what is only a fact-finding return to work interview.

For these reasons companies should ensure that their line managers understand the purpose of a return to work interview. If they stray from it, there may be expensive consequences if the employee subsequently issues proceedings in the employment tribunal.

● Wilful misconduct

There will be occasions when it is appropriate to use the disciplinary procedure. If it appears that there are no legitimate reasons for the employee's poor attendance or, on further investigation, the employer has reasonable grounds for suspecting that an employee is lying about the illness and wrongly claiming SSP (or company sick pay), then it is appropriate for a company to deal with the case through the disciplinary procedure.

Handling discipline is dealt with in Chapter 3.3 of the 2003/04 EEF Employment Guide (www.employmentguide.org.uk). In summary, where an employer suspects that an employee has lied about being ill and so fraudulently claimed SSP or company sick pay, the employer may consider summarily dismissing the employee for gross misconduct. Before doing so, the employer must have;

- carried out a reasonable investigation

- given the employee an opportunity to defend him or herself, and

- given the employee a right of appeal

otherwise the dismissal may be unfair. Also, from 1 October 2004, a dismissal will be automatically unfair if the employer has not followed the statutory discipline and dismissal procedure set out in summary on pages 27–31. This means writing to the employee explaining the reason why the employer is proposing to dismiss, holding a meeting with the employee to allow him or her to state his or her case, writing to explain the outcome and offering an appeal (see pages 27–31).

When to take formal action on the grounds of poor attendance

● Overview

If the company has an attendance management procedure, this should be followed. In this Guide we recommend that the procedure specifies the level of absence that triggers discussion with the employee. Managers should adhere to any triggers in individual cases to ensure consistency of treatment. If the company does not have any guidelines for triggering discussion, putting some in place should be a top priority for the manager responsible for managing attendance (see pages 35–6).

● Ensuring consistency of treatment

To ensure consistency of treatment (important in avoiding employment relations problems, ill feeling, grievances and, possibly, litigation) the company should set guidelines for the level of absence which would trigger each stage of its attendance management procedure. It is for each company to determine what these levels should be. Also, the triggers do not have to be uniform for the entire company (for example, the level of absence which might trigger action might be higher for delivery drivers if their absences cause proportionately more disruption). However, if different standards are applied to different classes of employee, then these must be clearly set out in writing and there should be some obvious logical reason for the difference. Managers must also be trained to apply these triggers consistently.

An attendance management procedure should, therefore, deal with these questions:

- what level of absence will trigger both informal and formal action?

- when is the slate wiped clean? That is, for how long must an employee sustain an improvement before the caution (or warning) expires? It is advisable to specify a time period, as with disciplinary warnings, and

- what happens if there is a relapse or an employee appears to be 'playing the system'?

Whatever arrangements are in place, there will often be employees who can work out exactly how much time they can take off before they trigger action, or they may improve for just sufficiently long for the slate to be wiped clean before attendance starts to fall off again. The procedure should, therefore, expressly give the employer the flexibility to trigger formal action if there are reasonable grounds, based on the pattern of absence, to consider that may be occurring.

● What kind of trigger – comparative or absolute?

A trigger does not have to be set as an absolute level of absence; it can be one relative to the attendance levels of other employees in the group. For example, employees with a Bradford score (see page 47) above the average for a defined group may become subject to review (see the case study on page 7 for an example of this). One advantage of setting comparative rather than absolute triggers is that it is harder for an employee to 'play the system'.

● Keeping triggers under review

Companies should keep their trigger levels under review. If they are not effective, or analysis shows that many employees appear to 'play the system' to their advantage, then they should be tightened. If the procedure is a contractual one then, in order to introduce new trigger levels, the company must follow the usual steps for changing contracts (see Chapter 5.1 'Changing contracts of employment' in the 2003/04 EEF Employment Guide, www.employmentguide.org.uk). In any event, we strongly advise that an attendance management procedure should not be part of the contract of employment (see pages 132–4).

Whether or not the procedure is contractual, all employees should be informed in writing of the triggers and the consequences for exceeding them as well as of any other changes (see pages 58–9).

● Do clearly defined triggers make dismissals on grounds of frequent short-term absence safe?

It is important to have trigger levels for taking action against employees on account of their attendance record because, if properly communicated, employees are aware of the consequences of further absence, and managers are more likely to act consistently. Both points are crucial ingredients in a fair dismissal. But, in considering the fairness of dismissal, tribunals look at all the circumstances of the particular case, including:

● length of service and past record

- reasons for the absence (including whether the absence is disability-related (see pages 157–9)). If the absence was caused by a work-related illness or injury, the tribunal can expect an employer to be more tolerant of the absence. If it is disability-related, the company may have to discount some or all of the absences as a reasonable adjustment (see pages 157–9)

- the actual detail of the attendance record (for example, if the employee had made substantial improvements and so had only just triggered the dismissal stage)

- the nature, length and effect of the illness and the prospects for improvement (this might require medical evidence (see pages 159–60))

- the effect of absence on the employer's operation and other employees, and

- any unusual factors, for example, if the post requires an employee to be in very good health.

From 1 October 2004, the company must also follow the statutory discipline and dismissal procedure otherwise a dismissal may be automatically unfair (see pages 27–31).

In short, a company should rely on trigger levels to review an employee's attendance record but not to trigger dismissal automatically. As tribunals also expect employers to act consistently, this puts the onus on employers to properly record the outcome of a review and, if a decision not to dismiss is taken, why. If a dismissed employee can point to another employee with a similar attendance record who was not dismissed, there is a risk of an unfair dismissal claim if the employer cannot demonstrate that it treated the employees consistently, even if the outcome of the review did not result in dismissal in both cases. This is a difficult balancing act but the key to success is good record keeping. Employers need to keep an accurate record of why a particular employee was not dismissed even though their absence exceeded a trigger level. The record may become important evidence if another employee who is subsequently dismissed brings unfair dismissal proceedings pointing to the 'leniency' afforded the first employee as an example of inconsistent treatment.

Should all short-term absences be counted when deciding whether to take formal action to manage the employee's absence record?

■ Absences which should always be excluded

When assessing whether an employee's attendance record is poor enough to warrant further action (including dismissal) the following absences (which are statutory entitlements) must be discounted[18]:

- pregnancy and maternity-related absence, including time off for ante-natal care

- time off for paternity, parental and adoption leave

- reasonable time off taken to deal with serious incidents involving dependants (although it is up to the employer to decide what is reasonable)

- time off for public duties

- time off for trade union duties or activities, and

- time off for young people studying or training for a specific qualification.

Perhaps the most difficult decision is assessing whether a tribunal would find the company in breach of its duty to make reasonable adjustments under the DDA if it failed to discount absences which relate to an employee's disability (see pages 157–9 below).

■ Treatment of disability-related absences

It is overstating the position to say all disability-related absences must be discounted, as the employer is only obliged to make reasonable adjustments to its trigger levels. Some of the factors the legislation allows employers to take into account when considering what is reasonable are set out on page 23. They include the size and resources of the employer. Also, an employer

---

18 See EEF Guide 'Family Leave and Flexible Working: An Employer's Guide'.

can only justify[19] failing to make such an adjustment if the employer's reason for dismissal (level of absence) is substantial, that is, the impact is more than minor or trivial, when all the circumstances are taken into account. This means that, what is reasonable for a small employer with a disabled employee in a key role (where absence can be highly disruptive) may differ from the level of absence the same employer could be expected to tolerate from, for example, a general administrative or production employee and may differ greatly from what a large employer could be expected to tolerate from a such a general employee.

As a minimum, employers will have to take into account the level of absence tolerated from other employees who do not have that disability, as the DDA Code of Practice (see page 18) illustrates:

'A factory worker with a mental illness is sometimes away from work due to his disability. Because of that he is dismissed. However, the amount of time off is very little more than the employer accepts as sick leave for other employees and so is very unlikely to be a substantial reason'.

We recommend that, as a minimum adjustment, employers discount the amount of absence related to a disability that would otherwise have triggered a first level caution. Whether a tribunal would consider that it would be reasonable for a company to make a more generous adjustment is an issue on which companies should seek further advice from their EEF Association, before the next stage of the procedure is reached. This is because of the near certainty that dismissal of a disabled employee on grounds of disability-related absence will result in a claim under the DDA (where unlimited compensation may be awarded) as well as a claim for unfair dismissal if the employee has at least one year's service. Remember, though, that an employee can also claim under the DDA that he or she has suffered a detriment if subjected to formal action short of dismissal so employers should seek advice at all stages and not just dismissal.

---

19 Note, however, that from 1 October 2004 it will no longer be possible to justify a failure to make reasonable adjustments; either an adjustment will be reasonable or it will not.

- Are there any other adjustments the employer should make for disability-related absences?

Employers should also investigate whether there are any aspects of the employee's work that makes working life difficult for the employee and may be a background factor for the sickness absence, as the following example illustrates.

Suppose a loud radio is played in the warehouse and an employee suffering from tinnitus working on the day shift has asked for it to be turned down to help relieve the symptoms. It is turned back up again for the night shift and the warehouse manager only turns it back down again in the morning when she remembers or the employee reminds her. The manager's failure to be mindful of this causes the employee to feel awkward and increasingly anxious. He starts taking time off sick, specifying the tinnitus.

In these circumstances, the reason for the employee's absence is reasonably within the employer's control. If a reasonable adjustment is made then the employer has to ensure that all relevant employees (usually the line manager, at least) are made aware of their responsibility to make sure the adjustment is effective (but bearing in the mind the duty to keep confidential an employee's medical condition (see page 54). Also, given the very high risk of a successful DDA claim, such absences should be discounted.

When should we seek medical advice in cases of frequent short-term absence?

Where an employee is dismissed for intermittent absences, an employment tribunal may be prepared to accept that there was no need for the employer to obtain medical evidence if the employee had had a series of unrelated short-term absences of a day or two here or there. This is because a doctor is unlikely to be able to provide useful information on the causes of these intermittent absences.

In the context of disability discrimination, however, an employer can be liable for discrimination if it dismisses or takes action short of dismissal against an employee for a reason relating to the employee's disability even if it is not aware that the individual is disabled. It is also under a duty to make reasonable adjustments for an employee if it either knows or could reasonably be expected to know that the employee is disabled.

Therefore, in practice, we advise always obtaining medical evidence before dismissal, to ensure that an employee with a record of intermittent absences does not have an underlying condition that may amount to a disability, such as clinical depression or a back injury. Practical guidance on obtaining medical information is set out on pages 93–8.

In relation to action short of dismissal, it is also wise to ask an employee with such a record if there is an underlying medical reason that the company should be aware of before taking the action (such as imposing a warning or caution). This does not provide a foolproof defence in the event that it subsequently emerges the employee had a disability but it does assist the employer to have asked the question. There may be other cases where the employer knows, or ought reasonably to know, that the employee does have a medical condition which might qualify under the DDA and in such cases it would be wise to seek medical advice and advice from your Association official before taking action short of dismissal too.

What procedural formalities should the company observe?

● Overview

It is a vital ingredient of a fair dismissal procedure that, where an employee's attendance record is giving cause for concern, the company has investigated the reason for the absence and informed (that is, warned or cautioned (see pages 149–53)) the employee that his or her attendance is being reviewed (thus giving him or her an opportunity to improve before being at risk of dismissal).

If a company routinely holds return to work interviews (as we recommend on pages 168–78), the first of these purposes, investigation of reasons for absence, will happen as a matter of course. As to the requirement that the employee be clearly told that his or her employment may be at risk if there is not a sustained improvement, we advocate in this Guide that routine return to work interviews are not used for this purpose. Thus the formalities we set out below do not apply to them.

- To what type of formal action connected with sickness absence do the statutory minimum procedural rules apply (from 1 October 2004)?

With the introduction from 1 October 2004 of statutory procedures intended to aid resolution of workplace disputes employers are likely to have to observe more stringent formalities than many will be used to. At the time of writing this Guide, the regulations confirming how the procedures will operate have not been finalised. We have taken into account what is certain when writing this Guide and indicated where there is presently doubt but we recommend that member companies seek advice on all dismissals in any event. The procedures also apply to certain types of action short of dismissal as set out below (and on pages 27–31).

The statutory discipline and dismissal procedure will not apply to action short of dismissal that takes the form of a warning. This includes a 'caution' under an attendance management procedure. It will, though, apply to other types of action short of dismissal such as:

- a disciplinary suspension without pay

- the withholding of sick pay for failure to comply with the company's absence notification rules, or

- a transfer or demotion

although these sanctions are only available to an employer who has expressly reserved in the contract the power to apply them or where the employee agrees to them.

The statutory rules must be complied with before the employer takes the action. The circumstances where they apply are illustrated below.

1 Dismissal

Suppose an employer operates a Bradford score system for triggering formal action by management if employees have a poor attendance record (see pages 47–8 and 153–6) and, despite informal counselling, followed by a first then second caution, an employee's attendance record has not improved. The next stage in the employer's attendance management procedure is dismissal. The statutory formalities now apply. In summary, to comply with them, the employer should write to the employee explaining the reason why it is proposing to dismiss, then meet with the employee to give him or her an opportunity to state his or her case. The employer should, therefore, write to the employee:

- stating the place, date and time of the meeting

- explaining that the purpose of the meeting is to consider his or her attendance record

- giving the details of the Bradford score, explaining how it is calculated and the dates of the absences[20] so that the employee can come to the meeting prepared to respond or explain his or her case

- enclosing a copy of the company's attendance management guidelines or procedure

- setting out details of the past action taken by the employer (dates of previous counselling/cautions) and explaining that, in view of the previous record, the outcome may be dismissal, and

- telling the employee of the statutory right to be accompanied.

The employer must also notify the employee in writing of the outcome and of his or her right of appeal. The employer should also follow any other rules set out in its own procedures.

2 Action short of dismissal

Suppose an employee fails to comply with the notification rules for absence and under the employer's disciplinary procedure this leads to a first written warning. In addition, the company sick pay scheme makes it clear that sick pay will not be paid for days where the employee has not complied with the notification requirements.

The employer is not obliged to follow the statutory procedure in relation to the warning but it must do so before concluding that it will withhold the sick pay.

However, in relation to the sick pay there will only be a penalty against the employer for failing to follow the statutory minimum procedure if the

---

20 The statute only requires the employer to 'inform' the employee of the grounds for taking action but we recommend that, to avoid doubt, this be put in writing.

employee successfully brings tribunal proceedings relating to it. The most likely claim would be a breach of contract and/or unlawful deduction from wages claim although it should be remembered that wrongly withholding pay could amount to grounds for resigning and claiming constructive dismissal.

The employee might bring a breach of contract/unlawful deduction claim if, for example, the notification rules are unclear, or there is a dispute as to whether the employee did in fact comply with them. If the employee's complaint is successful, the tribunal may award the employee not only the lost sick pay but also an enhancement of between 10 and 50% of it as a penalty against the employer for failing to follow the statutory procedure.

The difficulty is, the employer will not know in advance whether the employee will bring proceedings. Therefore, in the above case, the employer should follow the statutory procedure before withholding the sick pay. In practice, the disciplinary case is so intertwined with the issue of eligibility for sick pay that the employer would be advised to apply the statutory minimum rules to the warning stage of the disciplinary procedure too.

Because of these difficulties, we advise that, whenever an employee reaches the formal stages of the company's procedure (be it an attendance review or disciplinary procedure), the company should follow the statutory minimum procedure rules (as well as any more favourable company rules).

● Statutory right to be accompanied

All workers have the statutory right to be accompanied by a work colleague or certified trade union official of their choice at a disciplinary or grievance hearing, if they reasonably request to be. For these purposes, a disciplinary hearing is defined as a hearing that could result in the employer giving the worker a warning or taking some other action in relation to the worker. In addition, the right also applies to any meeting to which the statutory procedural rules applies (see pages 27–31).

In summary, this means a worker will have the statutory right to be accompanied at any meeting to discuss his or her sickness absence if the interview could result in the issuing of a warning that forms part of the employee's disciplinary record, or the imposition of some other form of sanction such as a caution. This includes informal counselling meetings which are recorded for the purposes of establishing that the next stage in any procedure is formal action for a particular employee. In effect, the courts treat such counselling meetings as the first stage of a formal procedure even though conventionally employers do not.

Assuming a company follows our recommendation to keep return to work interviews and meetings for formal action separate, the statutory right to be accompanied does not apply to fact-finding meetings such as a return to work interview called by the employer to investigate why an employee has been absent. The right to be accompanied would apply, though, if that meeting goes beyond an investigation into the reasons for the absence to consider what action to take against the employee, whether it is a disciplinary sanction or the imposition of some other sanction, such as a caution under an attendance management procedure (see pages 149–53).

It is for this reason that we strongly recommend that routine return to work interviews held after each and every absence are limited to fact-finding as set out on pages 151–2.

Companies may nevertheless wish, as a matter of good practice, to allow an employee to be accompanied at this type of interview, if he or she asks to be. If, though, the employer's internal procedures are more favourable, and allow a right to be accompanied or represented in such meetings, then this should be permitted, and the right brought to the employee's attention. This is especially important if the procedure forms part of the employee's contract of employment (although we do not recommend this (see pages 132–4)).

Rigorous notification procedures

● Objectives

Early and effective notification of absence helps employers to:

- plan as it gives the line manager the opportunity to gauge how long the employee may be away

- discourage casual absence, and

- in appropriate cases consider opportunities for rehabilitation, thereby potentially reducing the length of a particular absence.

Importance of clear rules

In many companies payment of company sick pay is dependent on the employee complying with the notification procedure – if the procedure is confusing there may be debate about whether someone has complied and so is entitled to sick pay (see pages 179–82).

How can notification rules reduce frequent short-term absence?

It is commonplace for employers to require employees to notify them if they are absent but it is the requirement that the employee notifies someone in authority, preferably the line manager, that discourages unnecessary absence (and the impact is enhanced if line managers rigorously conduct absence control interviews on return to work).

Meeting these objectives

In order to meet the objectives set out on page 164, rules about notification should contain the following features.

First contact

Save in real emergencies, employees must call personally, not use a proxy, otherwise the manager cannot discuss short-term rehabilitation steps such as adjusted duties.

Also, ideally, employees should have to contact their own line manager before the start of their working day (although this is not so essential if the line manager rigorously conducts return to work interviews). Most procedures require this but is it actually possible in practice? For example, if employees call before the start of their shift will the line manager be there to take the call? Will the switchboard be open? If they call at start time will managers often be in a meeting or out with clients?

If it is not practical, in the interests of clarity, the company should use a different notification procedure. For example, it may be better to designate one person to take calls and pass on messages and require line managers to call employees back to discuss the absence. Some companies require employees to call a dedicated answer-phone. Alternatively, line managers could be rotated on a duty desk to take calls from employees calling in sick. This method may be particularly useful in a production environment with lots of teams or cells.

Subsequent contact

To save managers constantly wondering: 'will the employee be in today?' it is better to require employees to make contact before every shift they miss unless otherwise agreed (for example, where it is clear that the employee will not be well enough to return to work before, say, next week).

How should we treat an employee who goes 'AWOL'?

There are three main responses the employer may want to consider:

- dismissal

- withholding sick pay for the period the employee has not been in contact with the company, and

- if the employee returns to work, disciplinary action short of dismissal for failing to notify the company (assuming the employee does not already have a disciplinary record which means the employee is at risk of dismissal).

We deal with these issues below.

Dismissal

An employment tribunal is very unlikely to consider it fair to dismiss an employee for failing to respond immediately to letters or phone calls on a day when he or she has not complied with the company's notification procedure. A prolonged period of unauthorised absence is, however, likely to give rise to circumstances in which the employer can fairly dismiss the employee.

However, in both cases, the employer must take steps to investigate the reason for the employee's conduct, give the employee an opportunity to explain him or herself and a right of appeal. The employer must also comply with the statutory minimum discipline and dismissal rules (from 1 October 2004 (see pages 27–31)) as well as any company procedural rules (particularly if they are contractual). It is not wise to assume the employee has resigned as this could result in a successful unfair dismissal claim.

We suggest that the employer take the following steps in the case of an employee who has not complied with the company's notification rules and cannot be contacted by telephone.

- The employer should write to the employee telling the employee that the absence is being treated as unauthorised, which is a serious disciplinary matter and which could lead to dismissal. If, however, the company's disciplinary procedure specifies a lesser sanction, this should be stated.

- The letter should set a time and place for a meeting giving a reasonable period of notice, and telling the employee of the statutory right to be accompanied.

At the time of writing, the Government has indicated that, under the statutory procedural rules coming into force on 1 October 2004, an employer must give an employee two chances (separated by a reasonable interval) to attend a hearing before proceeding to dismiss an employee in his or her absence. So, if an employee does not attend the first hearing, the employer must fix another one.

If the employer proceeds to dismiss in the employee's absence then it must, in compliance with the statutory minimum procedural rules write to the employee confirming that a decision to dismiss has been made and advising the employee of his or her right of appeal (see pages 27–31).

However, in our experience, it is rare for employees to go AWOL wilfully. It is worth making discrete enquiries of colleagues or trade union officials for further information. Even if the employer has complied with the statutory procedural rules, a tribunal may still find unfair a dismissal decision made in the employee's absence (under the ordinary law of unfair dismissal) if there was a serious and legitimate problem which prevented the employee making contact and which could have been easily ascertained (or was known of by other employees).

Sick pay and disciplinary action short of dismissal

An employer is entitled to withhold payment of SSP (or company sick pay if the contract specifies this) if its notification rules are not met and there was no good cause for the delay. Employees must be told what the rules are and there are certain limitations. If the company's rules for company sick pay do not specify that failure to comply with the requirements on notification will lead to payment being withheld it would be unwise to withhold payment unless the employee has failed to respond to the company's efforts to make contact. In any event the statutory minimum discipline and dismissal procedural rules will apply. Their application in these circumstances and to the disciplinary action is illustrated on pages 160–63.

Return to work interviews

■ Introduction

There is a limit to what absence statistics can tell a company. They don't paint a very accurate picture of the real causes of absences – whether it is genuine sickness, idleness or one of the underlying causes – many of which could be eliminated. What is effective is the return to work interview, where a manager discusses every single episode of absence with an employee on their return to work.

Return to work interviews encapsulate the key elements of a good strategy for maximising attendance. They:

- send a clear message to employees that the company takes absence seriously and discourages casual absence which is not genuine

- engage the line manager in managing the employee's attendance

- focus on the individual but allow management to see the bigger picture, if there is one

- remind employees they are accountable for their attendance record

- give employees the opportunity to raise problems/concerns which can be nipped in the bud, thereby reducing absence, and

- are a platform for further action, including rehabilitation (see below).

Why are return to work interviews effective?

If employees know that their absence is noticed, that it matters, and that some action will always be taken, standards do tend to improve.

Knowing that they will have to go through a return to work interview, over time, discourages employees from casual absence. Most people are basically honest. If, for example, there is a culture where employees see sick pay as an entitlement, a return to work interview can help break that culture down because employees have to look their manager in the eye and give them an explanation for their absence. If the illness is not genuine or is overstated, most people, eventually, will feel uncomfortable taking off 'unnecessary time'.

Managers who interview employees returning to work following sickness absence will develop a better understanding of the scale and nature of sickness absence within their team or department. In relation to individuals, a return to work interview may reveal underlying causes which are in the employer's control (see pages 170–73) or enable a manager to spot early a case which, if gone undetected and not referred for occupational health support, might lead to long-term ill-health absence.

These interviews are most effective if done quickly (preferably on the first day back) on the employee's return. If they are delayed, the manager has less opportunity to settle the employee back in and to check that he or she is fit to work. Line managers should only be permitted to delay the interviews where employees work remotely or there are other such special operational circumstances in which cases the interviews should still be conducted as soon as possible.

Establishing if the employee is fit enough to return to work

The manager may establish that the employee is not fit enough to return to work. In such cases, the employer should send the employee home again.

If there is a dispute about whether the employee is fit, the employer should seek advice. An employer who, without good reason, refuses to allow an employee to work who declares they are fit to do so will be acting in breach of contract, and so risking constructive dismissal complaints or a claim for unlawful deductions from wages for any lost pay (or a breach of contract claim on the same basis). This means the employer needs to seek the advice of an occupational health specialist or the employee's GP or specialist.

Employees who work when they are unfit can be a danger to themselves, their colleagues and customers/other members of the public. This means employers have to carefully balance their duty to allow fit employees to come to work (and so be paid) with their duty of care to the employee, his or her colleagues and others as well as their requirement under health and safety legislation to operate a safe system of work. Employers need occupational health advice in order to balance these obligations.

The employer could also be liable for the consequences of knowingly allowing an unfit employee to work if it caused or aggravated, for example, a stress-related disorder. This is because the courts have shown a willingness to recognise that some employees just do not know how to stop or 'say no'. Continuing to work may also, in the long-term, result in longer term absence for them. In other cases, allowing unfit employees to work could result in contagious diseases or viruses being spread throughout the workforce leading to other employees being absent.

● Asking what the problem is and respecting the employee's rights to medical confidentiality

When conducting return to work interviews line managers are seeking to encourage the employee to talk about the reason for the absence but they must also respect the wishes of employees who do not wish to disclose private medical information to their manager or team leader. The arrangements for conducting return to work interviews should also make it clear that such information can be given in confidence to, for example, the personnel function if there is one (see also page 173).

The manager conducting the return to work interview should therefore:

- explain that the interview is part of the company's arrangements for managing attendance

- set out its purpose

- explain that the employee does have to complete a self-certificate or provide a medical certificate (whichever is the case given the length of the absence)

- that the purpose of the interview is to discuss the absence but the employee is not required to tell the line manager if they do not want to the precise medical details, instead this can be given in confidence to whoever the company has nominated for this purpose.

This is an important issue to cover in the training of managers who conduct return to work interviews.

How should we respond if the employee reveals an underlying cause?

Employees are more likely to be forthcoming about the underlying causes of an absence when talking face to face to their manager than when completing a self-certificate. Also, managers are in a better position to do something – minimise or eliminate a problem – if they know what it is. For example:

- It may emerge that an employee is suffering from a serious medical condition. Taking some early rehabilitation steps may result in improved attendance and even prevent the employee going off on long-term sick leave.

- If there are underlying reasons for the absence that the company can control, this gives it an opportunity to deal with them. Examples might include health and safety issues including work-related stress disorders.

- It may become clear that some employees are using (paid) sick leave to cover what are essentially domestic emergencies for which they may be entitled to leave albeit unpaid under the statutory provisions for time off for dependants[21]. A return to work interview may help a manager to make it clear to the employee who has wrongly taken sick leave that this could

---

21 See EEF Guide 'Family Leave and Flexible Working: An Employer's Guide'.

be considered an abuse of the sick pay scheme with serious disciplinary consequences. Some employers may consider even a first offence of this sufficiently serious to warrant disciplinary action and even dismissal on the grounds of misconduct. The employer should also ensure that payroll knows that an overpayment of sick pay has been paid.

- Facts might emerge which suggest that changing working hours, job sharing, or allowing other flexible working options may be a solution if there are background factors such as travel difficulties, ill-health, or domestic difficulties, including childcare issues. There is no general legal duty to consider employee's requests for flexible working (although see below for the rights of parents). However, if the change is reasonable and there is a business case for making an adjustment, doing so may eliminate many episodes of short-term absence. If adjustments are made, they should be clearly documented, so that it is clear whether they are permanent or temporary and a review date should be agreed (see pages 101–102).

- Those employees with children under the age of 6 (18, if the child is disabled) in any event have a statutory right to request more flexible working arrangements (see page 186). Some employees (mainly but not exclusively women with children) may be able to make a claim under sex discrimination legislation if their employer cannot justify a refusal for more flexibility (such as part-time working (see footnote 16 on page 127)).

- The employer may have good reason to suspect the absence was not legitimate. For example, the employee may have just taken the odd day off work without authorisation, or have feigned ill-health to take advantage of the company's sick pay scheme, in which case the manager should trigger the disciplinary procedure (see pages 152–3).

- Steps can be taken to improve job design and working conditions and deficiencies in training and induction methods can be addressed. ACAS has produced guidance which deals in more detail with this aspect of managing some underlying reasons for absence[22].

22 'Absence and Labour Turnover' is available online at www.acas.org.uk/publications/b04.html.

◼ Link with harassment or dignity at work procedure

Employees may reveal facts that suggest that they are being bullied or harassed within the workplace. Again, if managers spot this early and tackle it an underlying cause of frequent short-term absence may disappear as morale improves.

If the employee reveals that his or her absence is due to stress caused by harassment or bullying, then the company will need to take steps to address that issue otherwise it risks a personal injury claim. If the harassment is on grounds of sex, race, sexual orientation or religion or is linked to the employee's disability, the employee could also allege unlawful discrimination. If the company takes no action to deal with it, or the steps it takes are inadequate, the employee could also decide to resign and claim unfair constructive dismissal.

There may be occasions where employees are reluctant to talk to their line manager about the reason for the absence. This may be because the line manager may be part of the underlying reason for it (for example, in cases of alleged bullying or harassment) or because the reason for the absence is very personal. This reticence may be acute where the employee and line manager are of the opposite sex. For this reason we suggest that a company include in its arrangements for return to work interviews the facility for employees, in defined circumstances, to speak instead to the personnel officer (or, if the member company does not have a dedicated personnel officer, a specified manager who has received relevant training which EEF can provide (see also pages 170–71)).

Return to work interviews should not be a substitute for, or the only mechanism for, monitoring anti-social behaviour in the workplace. An employee is not likely to raise issues of bullying and harassment if the interviewer, their line manager, is the perpetrator. We strongly recommend, therefore, that companies have in place a separate harassment or dignity at work policy which is brought to employees' attention.

◼ Taking further steps after a return to work interview

In many cases, the return to work interview may be just the first step. The next may be:

- a referral to occupational health and/or a request for further medical information from a GP or specialist

- consideration of rehabilitation

- disciplinary proceedings if the employee has abused the sick pay scheme by claiming sick pay when he or she was not ill

- further training and/or activation of a performance improvement procedure if the employee is struggling to do the job well

- an investigation into personality or culture issues such as racism, harassment, bullying or generally poor supervision

- carrying out a health and safety risk assessment

- consideration of altering working conditions or, if the employee qualifies for it (see page 186), activating the statutory procedure for considering requests for flexible working.

If the company's absence notification procedure is working well (see pages 164–7) line managers will usually know in advance of a return to work interview the reason the employee gave for the absence when calling in sick. The manager can then prepare (and, if necessary, take advice on) what the possible steps might be.

Conducting the return to work interview

- Before the meeting inform the employee of :
  - the time and venue
  - of the right to be accompanied if relevant (as long as the line manager sticks to the fact finding purpose of a return to work interview the statutory right does not apply (although the company may have granted more generous rights (see pages 163–4)).

- Be prepared:
  - take up to date attendance records to the meeting
  - check they are accurate
  - take along notes of previous return to work interviews
  - work out in advance what questions to ask (see below)

- consider what might be the next steps bearing in mind the reason for the latest absence, and the individual's attendance record
- where appropriate, contact before the interview other relevant colleagues (personnel function, occupational health services, Health & Safety, etc) to clarify in the line manager's mind the employee's rights/obligations and other sources of support.

- At the meeting:
  - explain the purpose of it
  - ask open ended questions to:
    - identify the problem/reason for the absence
    - establish if the problem is solved or the employee feels better
    - establish if the employee is, fit, safe and free from infection or contagious diseases (if relevant). This will involve asking the employee what their doctor has said to them
  - communicate any team/departmental or company news the employee may have missed
  - deal with allocation of work
  - record what was said
  - let the employee know he or she was missed
  - if further steps are necessary, inform the employee of that or tell the employee that he or she will be informed (soon) of any further steps if necessary.

Do's and Don'ts of a return to work interview

Do

- Interview:
  - every employee about every single episode of absence
  - on the day of his or her return.

Interview all employees in a team or department irrespective of the reason given for the absence when the employee phoned in sick. Inconsistency generates ill feeling, grievances and will be a relevant factor in dismissal and discrimination claims. Preferably all employees should be covered, including agency workers if, under its contractual arrangements with the agency supplying the workers, the client company has day- to-day control of them.

- Keep the interview:
  - brief
  - informal
  - private and free of interruptions.

- Have a simple pro forma for the manager to record the reason for the absence and other notes of the meeting. It may be helpful to have it printed on the back of a self-certificate form.

- If it is appropriate because of the level of absence give the employee informal counselling. The line manager should be specific and refer to actual records, rather than referring vaguely to the employee having 'too much time off'.

- Make a separate appointment to deal with further action if necessary (see pages 151–2).

Don't

- Make any exceptions.

- Interrogate or harangue the employee. Avoid a disciplinary tone, which would undermine the purpose of the interview (see pages 151–2).

- Be sarcastic but, if appropriate, remind the employee of his or her past record.

- Make value judgements about an employee's illness, particularly if it is a mental health problem.

  Managers must remember they are fact finding and not there to make value judgements about an employee's health or make comments about what is and isn't 'legitimate' sickness. Many employees, particularly those with mental health problems, can be very vulnerable to such value judgments, particularly from those in authority. Again, managers who are not clear of their role and who fall into this trap, expose the employer to litigation including work-related stress claims (or claims that work aggravated a non-work-related stress disorder) and claims under the DDA.

- Tag on other issues (except to explain what has happened in the team/ department during the absence and discuss work allocation). Don't use the opportunity to deal with misconduct or performance issues.

Training and support for managers in conducting return to work interviews

There is a danger that poorly trained managers or those with an overbearing manner may misunderstand the purpose of a return to work interview. The purpose of them is to instil a culture where employees think: 'Can I justify this?' before picking up the phone to call in sick. They are not intended to force sick employees to feel so guilty about being away that they struggle in, possibly under fear of reprisals.

Employers who intimidate sick employees into working expose themselves to a wide range of legal liability including breach of contract and constructive dismissal claims, work-related personal injury claims (including stress cases), and liability for failing to ensure a safe system of work under health and safety legislation. Also it is not good for morale or motivation.

There is a risk that line managers will see return to work interviews as a time-consuming and potentially embarrassing chore. They need to be properly trained to make sure the time spent is minimised and effective and when embarrassing issues come up, they know to whom they can turn for support. Issues to be covered in training include:

- Managers should know that they aren't expected to act as counsellors or psychotherapists, or to dispense occupational health or other medical advice. Their role is to establish the facts, and then, in conjunction with other colleagues (the personnel or HR function, occupational health, health and safety specialists, etc), to consider if any further steps are necessary.

- On the other hand, they must have sufficient training to be able to pick up on the warning signs of work-related issues such as evolving work-related stress, bullying, sexual or racial harassment, etc.

- Line managers may need support, particularly for dealing with difficult employees. Some employees may refuse to talk, or burst into tears or resent what they consider (wrongly) to be an intrusion into their privacy. The organisation MindOUT for mental health has produced a very useful resource pack for line managers which deals with such situations (see page 90).

● EEF training

EEF Associations can help companies to train their managers in effective return to work interviews (see page 7).

Spot checks at an employee's home

By this, we mean unannounced spot checks to establish whether the employee is truly at home sick. We deal separately with home visits for managing long term absentees for the purposes of keeping in touch (see pages 80–81).

This is a very resource intensive method and, in practice, is best reserved for cases where there is already a strong suspicion of gross misconduct.

In any event, employers should be wary of drawing the wrong conclusion if an employee is not at home. For example, modern medical advice to patients with back pain is to keep active and the employee could legitimately be out taking exercise. Employers would have to give employees the opportunity to state their case in the usual way in a disciplinary investigation before concluding that the employee was feigning illness.

If employers do conduct home visits they should be carried out with due regard to an employee's right to privacy and right to family life (see further pages 54–5, surveillance of employees).

Pre-employment screening

It is a myth that, since the advent of the DDA, employers are not entitled to ask about or take into account an employee's absence record with a previous employer. Yes, there are pitfalls in doing so now but, if approached carefully and with due regard to the requirements of the DDA, not employing employees who have unacceptable levels of absence with a previous employer can be an effective method of reducing absence.

There are two aspects to pre-employment screening:

- establishing whether the applicant has health problems that mean he or she would not be fit to do the job or might be made worse by the job, and

- establishing whether the employee has a poor sickness absence record and is, therefore, a bad risk. Generally speaking, a short-term absence sickness record over the past two years is a good indication of the likely pattern over the next two years.

Employers should be asking for information from job applicants about both aspects. The assessment should be carried out by an occupational health professional, who is fully aware of the employer's obligations under the DDA.

The medical information and any supporting medical information from the applicant's GP or specialist should remain confidential to the occupational health physician advising the company. There is no reason, though, why the employer should not see the information about absence records but should seek the advice of the occupational health physician on whether there is an underlying cause for a particular pattern which might indicate a disability under the DDA. This may mean that the applicant should be referred to the company doctor for an assessment (see pages 61–9).

Controls in sick pay schemes

General principles

When employers are drawing up or revising a sick pay scheme there are a number of policy decisions they have to make. Relevant issues are summarised in paragraph 3.2.45-3.2.54 of the 2003/04 EEF Employment Guide, (see also www.employmentguide.org.uk). Companies should also consider if there are any controls that it could be appropriate for them to include in their schemes to help them tackle frequent short-term absence.

Some of the most frequently used controls for this purpose are:

- Requiring employees to serve 'waiting days' before they become eligible for sick pay. An employer needs to decide if this requirement is to apply to all employees or only certain categories; and if so, for how many days?

- Providing that sick pay is not payable in certain specified circumstances such as whilst the employee is working out his or her notice or whilst the employee is subject to disciplinary proceedings. Some companies who use a Bradford Score system provide that, after a certain level of absence, sick pay is not payable. If employees are excluded in certain circumstances, sick pay schemes must be drafted to make this very clear and should be brought to their notice (see pages 58–60).

- Providing that sick pay is discretionary. Again this policy could be applied to all employees or could be limited to specified circumstances (such as those mentioned in the point above). Remember, though, that if the employer has discretion as to whether it pays sick pay, it is under an implied contractual obligation to exercise that discretion rationally. It is also advisable to set out guidance to managers on the exercise of that discretion (whilst making it clear that the guidance is not exhaustive) to ensure that they treat employees equitably. If the employer decides to exercise its discretion not to pay sick pay for a reason relating to the employee's conduct (such as failure to comply with notification rules) or capability (such as the submission of a vague medical certificate (see pages 120–22)) the employer must apply the new statutory procedural rules (from 1 October 2004) before stopping pay

- Expressly providing that sick pay is only payable if the employee has fully complied with the company's notification procedures, and

- Expressly providing that the company has the right to terminate the contract, whether because of sickness absence or for any other reason, before sick pay has been exhausted.

In our view, ensuring there are controls to deal with frequent short-term absence provides an important safety net for companies. However, they are not necessarily a substitute for managing each individual case of frequent short-term absence and taking the other measures we advocate in this Guide. The operation of these controls also involves significant legal issues (for example, the requirement that employers exercise their discretion rationally). They also raise significant employee relations issues and employers need to ensure that these provisions fit with their overall policy on setting terms and conditions (particularly if certain categories of employees are to be treated differently).

We also consider below another possible control, that is a requirement on employees to provide a doctor's certificate for an absence of less than eight days.

● Requiring a doctor's certificate for all sickness absences, irrespective of length

It is a myth that an employer cannot require medical certificates for absences of less than 8 days and so employees can only self-certificate. However, it is the case that:

- Employers cannot make production of such a medical certificate a condition of qualification for SSP, only company sick pay. Assuming all the other qualifying conditions are met, an employee will be entitled to SSP as long as he or she provides a self-certificate for absences of less than 8 days.

- Under GP's terms of service with the NHS, they are not required to issue (and are not paid for issuing) medical certificates for short-term sickness absence. But if they do, they can charge a private fee (the current recommendation of the BMA is £9).

- To issue a medical certificate GPs must normally have examined the employee on the date of issue or the day before. This means they are not allowed to 'back-date' medical certificates unless the doctor has clear clinical evidence that, if the employee had asked for a medical certificate on a particular date, the doctor could have advised staying off work and for the whole of the period of the certificate. This is highly unlikely to be the case for minor illnesses. This can present employees with serious practical problems if they have a short-lived illness and there are long waiting times for appointments at their surgery.

- Given the cost of a medical certificate the employer will meet considerable union and/or employee resistance for such a policy and may come under pressure to pay for them. The employer is not obliged to pay though.

On the other hand, some companies who insist on medical certificates often report it is a very effective policy for reducing casual absence.

There is unease, though, that employers who require medical certificates for even short-term absence are placing an unnecessary burden on GP services. In 2002, the Cabinet Office estimated that such employers were responsible for more than 2 million unnecessary GP appointments and advocated instead that employers actively manage short-term sickness absence, particularly by using return to work interviews (see pages 168–78).

If an employer does decide to require medical certificates for absences of less than 8 days, it might consider only applying the policy to:

- employees who, as a group, have higher than average absence levels and/or whose absence causes the most disruption and/or

- individual employees with a poor short-term absence level (as triggered by, for example, a defined Bradford score) although employers should seek advice in relation to employees who are or might be protected by the DDA.

In any event, the company's sick pay rules should:

- clearly state when a medical certificate is required (or, if the company wishes to retain the discretion to require one at any time, that is clearly stated)

- spell out if the employee has to pay for the certificate

- specify the timescale for submitting it

- specify to whom it should be submitted, and

- spell out the consequences if an employee does not produce one (that is, if relevant, disqualification from sick pay for that period).

Inducements

● 'Good attendance' letters

As well as focussing on those employees with a poor attendance record, a comprehensive attendance management approach should provide some mechanism for acknowledging the efforts of good attendees. Some companies do this by sending employees 'good attendance' letters or raising it as a specific issue in appraisals and find that such initiatives are well received by employees.

● Attendance bonuses

Some companies find that a positive financial incentive is effective in maintaining high attendance levels. Indeed, many companies that consolidate attendance bonuses often find absence levels creep up unless remedial steps, such as adopting return to work interviews, are also taken. To other companies the idea of an attendance bonus is anathema, and they would consider it tantamount to 'paying employees twice' to come to work.

Those companies considering paying an attendance-related bonus should bear the following points in mind:

● to be effective, the bonus arrangements must be simple, transparent and of a sufficient amount to make a difference. If it is not, the company will have to bear the costs of administering the scheme for no real benefit.

● Employers must ensure that they make reasonable adjustments to ensure that employees with disabilities are not disadvantaged by the qualifying conditions for a bonus.

● Similarly, employees taking statutory leave such as maternity leave, time off for dependants, etc should not be prejudiced. Their time on the leave should be excluded from the reckoning and should not be counted in establishing whether the employee has attained any minimum threshold of attendance to qualify for a bonus at all.

Making sure bonus schemes do not unlawfully discriminate (either directly or indirectly) against certain categories of employees can be a difficult issue on which member companies affected should seek advice from their EEF Association.

● Can we reduce the holiday entitlement of employees with a poor attendance record?

Under the Working Time Regulations 1998 employees have an absolute entitlement to four weeks paid holiday which entitlement cannot be reduced except in the last year of employment. Employers cannot pro rate this entitlement on the grounds of absenteeism, including long-term absence. So, in the case of a worker covered by relevant provisions of the EEF National Agreement, where holiday entitlement is reduced after 13, 26 and 39 weeks' absence, an employer would not be able to rely on the Agreement to reduce the statutory entitlement. Therefore, a worker who was off work for, say, 40 weeks, would still be entitled to take his or her statutory annual leave of four weeks (inclusive of statutory holidays). It should be noted that any contractual leave over and above the statutory minimum can be reduced in the contract, as was the case before the working time legislation came into force.

Team competition and absence 'league tables'

Many companies generate internal competition as a way of improving morale and motivating employees to reach higher performance levels. Some companies add absence levels to the equation, perhaps producing 'league tables' of attendance, which are made public, via e-mail or notice boards.

Experience shows this can be a very effective mechanism for discouraging casual absence and motivating line managers to manage attendance more effectively. There are dangers, though, if, for example, team leaders do not recognise the dividing line between healthy peer pressure to discourage casual absence and inappropriate peer or management pressure on individuals who have genuine ill-health difficulties. Managers must be trained to spot the difference. The latter can contribute to work-place injuries (including work-related or work-aggravated stress claims) and harassment claims by individuals who may have protection under the DDA.

Some employers go so far as to identify individuals and their levels of absence, 'naming and shaming' rather than using just aggregate figures for a cell or team. In our view, and that of the Information Commissioner, this is unlawful (see pages 52–4) and, in any case, is of dubious motivational value.

Whilst team competition, and a focus on absenteeism in particular, can discourage casual absence, it is important to ensure that any benefits gained are not cancelled out by an increase in the number of days lost through workplace injuries caused by managers and employees cutting corners on health and safety in pursuit of, for example, the highest production figures.

Making attendance count in employment decisions

As long as the company does not overstep the mark and unlawfully penalise employees for pregnancy-related absence (or other statutory reasons for taking time off – see pages 155–9) or unlawfully take into account absence related to a disability (see pages 19–20), emphasising that frequent short-term absence is detrimental to career prospects can be influential on some employees and help foster a culture of good attendance. A company could make it clear to employees that it will take into account an employee's attendance level in considering applications for promotion, in appraisal decisions, payment of performance-related pay (see also Attendance bonuses above) and, of course, selection for redundancy purposes. This could be done in writing by way, for example, of a general statement in the company handbook and highlighted in an induction course, as well as being spelled out in any relevant policy (which should be the case in any event in a redundancy selection procedure, appraisal or performance pay scheme).

Employers should bear in mind that, applying such a policy in the case of employees who have a personal injury claim pending against the company for a work-related illness or injury may be adding to its liability costs. This is a matter they should take up with their advisers on such claims. They should also take advice from their EEF Associations in relation to employees who qualify (or who may qualify) for protection from discrimination under the DDA. Your EEF Association can advise on appropriate wording and implementation, taking into account the points above.

In practice, such measures do more to reward good attendees than motivate poor attendees to improve their record. They also depend on good record keeping although employers should be keeping these any way (see Step 2).

Flexible working

Employers are under a duty to make reasonable adjustments to the working arrangements of a disabled person disadvantaged by them and employees with children under six (18 if disabled) have the right to request more flexible working arrangements. There may also be a requirement under sex or race discrimination legislation or legislation prohibiting discrimination on the grounds of religion or belief to consider more flexible working arrangements. For more details on employees' family-related rights see EEF Guide 'Family Leave and Flexible Working: An Employer's Guide'.

There is not, however, a general requirement to consider more flexible working arrangements for employees who are sick or injured (although, in practice, employment tribunals expect employers to have considered them before deciding to dismiss an employee on capability grounds).

We do, however, recommend that employers consider temporary modifications to working arrangements where they can be accommodated even for employees who do not have a legal right to them as such measures can significantly reduce short-term absenteeism where there is a clear cause, such as domestic difficulties.

Employee health initiatives

Employers who participate in health promotion campaigns are helping, albeit indirectly, to cut down on both short and long-term absence. These initiatives need not be costly to the employer; they are also very popular with employees and give a clear indication to them that the employer cares about their well-being. Examples include health promotion activities for:

- Healthy hearts
- Healthy backs

- Lifestyle programmes

- Alcohol and addiction programmes

Where these initiatives involve screening, they can pick up significant diseases even if they have not yet caused symptoms in an employee. For example, identifying a severely high blood pressure may save that person's life. They can also educate employees in measures to prevent the development of disease as they get older.

Further detail on employees' rights on dismissal (see page 31)

Right of appeal

If the circumstances are so serious that the employer concludes there is no alternative but dismissal, the employee must be given a right of appeal. This is already an essential aspect of a fair dismissal process but, from 1 October 2004, it will be mandatory to do this.

The letter of dismissal, therefore, should:

- state that the employee has the right to appeal the decision

- give the employee a deadline for telling the employer if he or she intends to exercise the right, and

- state the employee must notify the employer in writing if he or she intends to appeal and set out the grounds of appeal in writing. If the employee does not have to give the grounds at the same time as notifying the employer he or she intends to appeal, this should be made clear in the letter, setting out the second deadline.

Unless the contract says otherwise, as with dismissals for disciplinary reasons, the employer can give notice of dismissal before the appeal has been heard. In ill-health absence cases, we suggest employers consider waiting until after an appeal has been heard particularly if the employee has already run out of sick pay. If, however, the employee is covered by EEF national procedural agreements, he or she is entitled to call for an external conference and to remain in employment until agreement is reached or the procedure is exhausted or his or her notice expires, if that is later.

Hearing the appeal

Wherever possible, the appeal should be heard by someone who was not involved in the original decision to dismiss.

The employee has the statutory right to be accompanied at any appeal hearing by a work colleague or certified trade union official if he or she wishes to be (although the employer's internal procedure may specify a wider category of companions or allow for actual representation).

Pay during notice period

An employee who is dismissed or resigns with notice while on sick leave may have the right to be paid his or her usual pay during the period of notice, even if that falls during a time when he or she would otherwise have received less than full pay, or no pay at all if the employee's sick pay entitlement has run out. Employees have this right if they are contractually entitled to no more than six days more than the minimum notice of dismissal required by the Employment Rights Act 1996 otherwise the right does not apply. The minimum is, broadly speaking, one week for each year that the employee has been employed in the company, up to a maximum of 12 weeks. So, for example, if an employee with seven years' service has a contractual entitlement to three months' notice then the statutory right to pay during notice does not apply.

If, by the time notice starts to run, the employee has exhausted company sick pay, the company should consider reclassifying the employee's status so that it is clear that they are receiving 'sick' pay again during the notice period. This is because the legislation allows an employer to offset against the notice pay due any state benefits that the employee may be receiving as long as the employee is technically in receipt of 'sick pay' during the notice period and the contract allows the employer to make the offset.

Pay in lieu of notice

The company may prefer to dismiss the employee with immediate effect. In that case, it should ensure that it makes the employee a payment in lieu of notice that fully reflects the pay and other benefits the employee would have received during his or her notice period. The employee would also still be entitled to an appeal against dismissal (see above).

Other contractual rights

An employer must take care when dismissing an employee not to breach any contractual rights otherwise it risks a claim for wrongful dismissal. If the employee is entitled to sickness benefits under the contract, it is very likely wrongful for the company to dismiss before those benefits are exhausted, unless the contract makes clear that the company has the right to do so (see page 109).

Given the risk of substantial wrongful dismissal claims, employers should seek advice from their EEF Association before dismissing for any reason a sick employee whose terms and conditions or the Company's handbook refer to long term sick or disability benefits (such as a PHI scheme).

Written reasons for dismissal

An employee who has been employed for one year or more at the time when he or she is dismissed is entitled to ask for a written statement of the reasons for his or her dismissal. This right also applies if the employee worked under a fixed-term contract that the employer has decided not to renew. The request need not be in writing. An employee who is dismissed while she is pregnant or during the first 26 weeks of her maternity leave is entitled to written reasons for her dismissal regardless of her length of service and without having to request them.

The company must provide the written reasons for dismissal within 14 days of receiving the employee's request. If it wishes, it can send the employee a copy of a previous statement or letter setting out the reasons for dismissal. The statement of reasons that the company gives is admissible in evidence in any legal proceedings and so it could be referred to if the employee claims that his or her dismissal was unfair.

A hypothetical example of the use of certain management tools for analysing attendance records

In this Appendix we give an illustration of the application of the management tools described in Step 2 (pages 45–8) for analysing absence information.

In the table is aggregate data for a number of departments in a hypothetical organisation. This data suggests the following:

- Department 1 has a large number of employees from the total workforce who have frequent short-term absences (high Bradford score, low duration and high severity rate). The company might consider prioritising this department when it rolls out a programme of return to work interviews.

- Department 2 has a number of employees who have had long absence durations (a high severity rate and a low Bradford score). This suggests management has been passive in managing long-term absences. The company should consider organising case management reviews (see pages 75–80) and a reference to an occupational heath adviser to assess prospects for rehabilitation (see also the case study on page 7).

- Departments 2 and 3 have very similar results except for the high Bradford score in Department 3; this suggests there is a fair amount of short-term absence.

- Department 4 is exceptional because it has very low severity rates as well as a low Bradford score (an ideal situation requiring further investigation into the cause of this encouraging result). Lessons and experience can be shared with managers in other departments.

- Department 5 has a small number of employees from the total workforce who have frequent short absences (the absence rate is low but the Bradford score is high).

Department	Type of employee	Severity (lost time as a percentage) %	Severity (lost time per employee in days)	Frequency (spells per employee)	Frequency (percentage of employees having at least 1 spell during the year) %	Duration (days absent per spell)	Average of Bradford score for the department
1	Manual	6.3	14.4	2.9	86	4.9	633
2	Non-manual	4.6	10.5	1.4	74	7.8	76
3	Manual	4.2	9.5	2.0	67	4.8	382
4	Non-manual	0.8	1.8	0.8	45	2.2	42
5	Non-manual	2.8	6.3	1.0	55	6.0	16

About EEF

EEF, the manufacturers' organisation, has a membership of 6,000 manufacturing, engineering and technology-based businesses and represents the interests of manufacturing at all levels of government. Comprising 11 regional Associations, the Engineering Construction Industries Association (ECIA) and UK Steel, EEF is one of the UK's leading providers of business services in employment relations and employment law, health, safety and environment, manufacturing performance, and education and skills.

EEF Regional and affiliated Associations

East Anglia

32 High Street, Hadleigh, Ipswich IP7 5AP

Tel: 01473 827894

Fax: 01473 824218

East Midlands & Mid-Anglia

Barleythorpe, Oakham, Rutland LE15 7ED

Tel: 01572 723711

Fax: 01572 757657

54 High Street, Sandy, Bedfordshire SG19 1AJ

Tel: 01767 681722

Fax: 01767 691773

ECIA

Broadway House, Tothill Street, London SW1H 9NS

Tel: 020 7799 2000

Fax: 020 7233 1930

Northern

Derwent House, Town Centre: District 1, Washington,

Tyne & Wear NE38 7SR

Tel: 0191 416 5656

Fax: 0191 417 9392

Northern Ireland

2 Greenwood Avenue, Belfast BT4 3JL

Tel: 02890 595050

Fax: 02890 595059

North West

Mount Pleasant, Glazebrook Lane, Glazebrook, Warrington WA3 5BN

Tel: 0161 777 2500

Fax: 0161 777 2522

Scottish Engineering

105 West George Street, Glasgow G2 1QL

Tel: 0141 221 3181

Fax: 0141 204 1202

Sheffield

Broomgrove, 59 Clarkehouse Road, Sheffield S10 2LE

Tel: 0114 268 0671

Fax: 0114 266 4227

South

Station Road, Hook, Hampshire RG27 9TL

Tel: 01256 763969

Fax: 01256 768530

Western

Engineers' House, The Promenade, Clifton Down, Bristol BS8 3NB

Tel: 0117 973 1471

Fax: 0117 974 4288

West Midlands

St James's House, Frederick Road, Edgbaston, Birmingham B15 1JJ

Tel: 0121 456 2222

Fax: 0121 454 6745

Yorkshire & Humberside

Fieldhead, Thorner, Leeds LS14 3DN

Tel: 0113 289 2671

Fax: 0113 289 3170

SEMTA (EEF strategic partner)

(Sector Skills Council for Science, Engineering, Manufacturing and Technology)

14 Upton Road, Watford, Herts WD18 0JT

Tel: 01923 238441

Fax: 01923 256086

Index

absence information
    analysing 45–8
    Bradford score 8, 45, 47–8
    Data Protection Act (1998) 44–5
    vs. health information 43–4
    record-keeping 44–8
absence league tables 184–5
absence reduction, case study 7–14
Access to Medical Reports Act
  (1988) (AMRA) 51–2
Access to Work Scheme (AWS) 66–7
accompanied, right to be 31, 163–4
adjustments, reasonable *see*
  reasonable adjustments
AMRA *see* Access to Medical Reports
  Act (1988)
analysing
    absence information 45–8
    attendance records 45–8, 148,
      192–3
appeal rights 29, 188–9
assessment
    medical information 99
    risk 42, 104
assistance, EEF Associations 7

Association of Chartered
  Physiotherapists in Occupational
  Health 69
attendance management policy
  132–4
attendance records
    analysing 45–8, 184, 192–3
    see also absence information
AWOL, employee going 166

back pain, case study 134–6
barriers to rehabilitation 111–30
benefits, contractual ill-health
  benefits 109
bonuses, attendance 183–4
Bradford score, absence information
  8, 45, 47–8
business case for rehabilitation 70–1

calculating cost of absence 41–2
case management
    handling medical cases 75–80
    line managers 75–80
    medical certificates 82–3
    rehabilitation 75–80

case study 7–14, 134–44
    absence reduction 7–14
    disciplinary proceedings 142–4
    EEF member company 7–14
    lower back pain 134–5
    stress 136–42
catastrophic illness 111
CBT *see* cognitive behavioural
  therapy
certificates, medical *see* medical
  certificates
changing company policy 130–1
checklists
    attendance management policy
      132–4
    obtaining medical information
      95–8
    rehabilitation measures 86–9
Code of Practice
    disability discrimination 18, 85
cognitive behavioural therapy (CBT)
  91
colleagues' reaction to rehabilitation
  14, 73–4
company sick pay
    changing policy 131
    controls in 179–82
    notice period 189–90
    rehabilitation and 127–9
    withholding 28, 121, 94, 122,
      124–6, 162–3, 166–8, 179–82
confidentiality
    health information 50–5
    occupational health professionals
      50–1

privacy 54–5
    return to work interviews 170
conflicting medical evidence 99–100
consent, medical information 51–2,
  93–4
consistency of treatment
    formal action 154
    paying for treatment 92
consultation, rehabilitation
    employees 83–4, 100–1
    representatives 56–60, 131–1
contacting
    employees 80–2, 87
    employee's GP/specialist 95
    notification procedures 165–6
contract of employment, company
  sick pay 121–2, 124
contracts of employment 56, 59
    changing policy and 130–4
contractual ill-health benefits 109
costs, absence 41–2

Data Protection Act (1998) 36
    absence information 44–5
    health information 52–4
    obligations 52–3
    storing health information 54
DDA *see* Disability Discrimination
  Act
DEAs *see* Disability Employment
  Advisers
delays, NHS delays 90, 130
dignity at work procedure 173
disability definition 17, 98, 108–9
    doctor's opinion 98

disability discrimination 15–26
    Code of Practice 18, 85
    defining 17–20
    less favourable treatment 18–20
    reasonable adjustments 19–24,
        106, 159
    Workplace (Health, Safety and
        Welfare) Regulations (1992) 24
Disability Discrimination Act (DDA)
    15–26, 85
    barrier to rehabilitation 113–14
    compliance 106
    employers' concerns 113–14
    qualification under 16–17, 98,
        113–14
    reasonable adjustments 19–24,
        106, 159
    rehabilitation 16–20
    unfair dismissal 16
Disability Employment Advisers
    (DEAs) 66
disability-related short-term absence
    157–9
disciplinary action
    contrasted with cautions 148–51
    notification procedures 166–8
    sickness during, case study 142–4
    short-term absence 148–67
discipline
    EEF Employment Guide 153
    notification 166–8
    statutory procedural rules 27,
        126, 160–3
dismissals
    deciding on 108–9, 166–8

frustration of contract 26
    notification procedures 166–8
    pregnancy-related absence 27
    reluctant employees 126–7
    rights 187–9
    short-term absence 25–6, 153–
        64, 166–7
    statutory procedural rules 27,
        126, 160–3
    summary of employees'
        entitlement 31–2
    unfair dismissal 16, 24–5,
        104–11
    warnings 106–7
    written reasons 190
documenting see record-keeping
duty
    reasonable adjustments 19,
        20–4, 106–7, 155–9
    trust and confidence 54

early intervention, rehabilitation
    72
early retirement, ill-health 109–11
EEF Employment Guide
    accessing health information
        51–2, 54
    adjustments, reasonable 21
    contract of employment 56
    defining disability 17
    discipline 153
    inform/involve workforce 59, 60
    notification procedures 56
    sick pay 179–80
    SSP 94

employees
  accessing own health
    information 54
  accompanied, right to be 31,
    163–4
  catastrophic illness 111
  consultation, rehabilitation 83–4,
    100–1
  contact, maintaining 80–2
  contacting workplace 87
  dignity at work procedure 173
  harassment 81–2, 173
  health initiatives 186
  involving and informing 56–60
  monitoring progress 102–3
  privacy 54–5
  reluctant rehabilitation 122–9
  retirement 109–11
  spot checks 55, 178
  statutory procedural rules 27–30,
    126, 160–3
  surveillance 54–5, 178
  visiting workplace 87
Employers' Forum on Disability 69

failure, rehabilitation 104–11
flexible working 186
flow chart, handling medical cases
  76–8
formal action
  case study 11
  consistency of treatment 154
  return to work interviews 151–2
  short-term absence 148–67
  triggers 154–6

types 149–53
when to take 153–6
formalities, procedural, short-term
  absence 160–4
frequency of absence 46
frustration of contract, dismissals 26

'good attendance' letters 183
GPs
  company sick pay 124–5
  medical certificates 115–22,
    181–2
  medical information 95–8
  rehabilitation 127
  reluctant employees 127
grievance, statutory procedural rules
  27

handling health information 50
handling medical cases 75–80
harassment
  of sick employees 81–2, 173
  reason for absence 172–3
health and safety requirements
  disabled employees 24
  representatives 39
  risk assessments 42, 104
health information
  accessing 51–2
  analysing 48–9
  confidentiality 50–5
  Data Protection Act (1998) 52–4
  handling 50
  monitoring 48–55
  reasons for monitoring 48

rights 50–5

storing 54

vs. absence information 43–4

health initiatives, employees 186

health professionals

confidentiality 50–1

see also occupational health

professionals

holiday entitlement, employees 184

HR function see personnel function

Human Rights Act (1998), privacy

54–5

identifying, attendance problem 8–9

ill-health

early retirement 109–11

illness, catastrophic 111

impeding recovery, rehabilitation

103

inducements, good attendance

183–4

inform/involve workforce 57–8

inform/involve workforce 56–60

individual employee notification

60

induction 57–8

legal obligations 59

notification procedures 56–7

strategy 4

written attendance management

policy 59

injury, work-related personal injury

129

interviews see return to work

interviews

job protection 127–9

league tables, absence 184

less favourable treatment

defining 18–20

disability discrimination 18–20

justifying 19–20

line managers

case management 75–8

personnel function 37–8

resource pack, mental health 90

roles 34–5, 36–7, 71–3

long-term absence, case studies 7,

134–44

lower back pain, case study 134–5

management

line managers 34–5, 36–7, 71–3

rehabilitation 101–4

reluctant managers 112–14

roles 34–9, 71–3

senior managers 34–6

support 177–8

training 177–8

management tools, analysing

attendance records 148, 192–3

medical advice, short-term absence

159–60

medical cases, handling 75–8

medical certificates

culture, sick note 115–17

for all absences 181–2

GPs 115–22, 181–2

long-term absence 117–19

prompt for rehabilitation 82–3

vague 119

medical evidence
  conflicting 99–100
  implications 100
  sufficient 107–8
medical information 93–8
  assessing 99
  checklist 95–8
  consent 93–4
  GPs 95–8
  obtaining 93–8
  receiving good 95–8
medical treatment, paying for 90–3
Mental Health Foundation
  MindOUT 90
  resource pack 90
MindOUT, resource pack 90
mobility, rehabilitation 89
monitoring
  absence 43
  employees' progress 102–3
  health information 48–55
MRI scanning 91

New Deal for Disabled People 67
NHS delays 90, 130
NHS Plus 68
notice period
  company sick pay 189
  pay in lieu of notice 189–90
notification procedures
  AWOL 166
  disciplinary action 167
  dismissals 166–7
  EEF Employment Guide 56

first contact 165
  importance 165
  inform/involve workforce 56–7
  objectives 164
  reducing short-term absence
    165
  short-term absence 165–7
  SSP 167

occupational health advice,
  accessing 61–9, 112
occupational health professionals
  confidentiality 50–1
  pre-employment screening 62–3
  rehabilitation 127
  reluctant employees 123–4,
    127
  risk reduction 62
  support 61–4
occupational health support see
  support

pace of work, rehabilitation 88
patterns of work, rehabilitation 87
pay see company sick pay; statutory
  sick pay
paying for treatment
  rehabilitation 90–3
  tax liability 92–3
penalties, non-compliance, statutory
  procedural rules 30
phased return to work 87
physiotherapists, Association of
  Chartered Physiotherapists in
  Occupational Health 69

policy
    attendance management and
        rehabilitation 132–4
    case study 7–14
    changing 130–1
poor attendance *see* short-term
  absence
pre-employment screening 178–9
    occupational health professionals
        62–3
pregnancy-related absence 27
    dismissals 27
privacy *see* confidentiality; Data
  Protection Act (1998)
procedural formalities
    short-term absence 160–4
    see also notification procedures
procedural rules, statutory *see*
  statutory procedural rules

qualification under DDA 17, 98,
  113–14

reasonable adjustments
    DDA 15–26
    duty 19, 20–4, 106, 159
    failure to make 24
record-keeping
    absence information 44–8
    health information 48–54
    rehabilitation arrangements
        101–2
    return to work interviews
        174–5
    statutory procedural rules 31

rehabilitation 70–144
    adapting work content 88
    aims 70
    barriers 111–12
    business case for 70–1
    case management 75–80
    checklist for policy 132–4
    colleagues, impact on 73–4
    DDA, overlap with 16–20
    documenting 101–2
    early intervention 72
    employee consultation 83–4
    extra training 89
    failure 104–11
    government support 66
    GPs 127
    help with transport 89
    impeding recovery 103
    inappropriate 104–11
    integrating existing policy 130–4
    legal requirement 16
    line managers' role 71–3
    measures 86–9
    medical conflict 127
    mobility 89
    occupational health professionals
        127
    pace of work 88
    patterns of work 87
    paying for treatment 90–3
    phased return to work 87
    in practice 74–111
    record-keeping 101–2
    review dates 103–4
    risk assessments 104

special treatment 72–4

strategy 5–6

trade union response 131

visiting workplace 87

workplace adaptation 88–9

relapses, preventing 102–3

reluctant employees 122–9

dismissals 126–7

reluctant managers 112–14

retirement, ill-health early retirement 109–11

return to work interviews

conducting 174–5

confidentiality 170

dignity at work procedure 173

do's and don'ts 175–6

effectiveness 169

establishing employee's fitness 169–70

formal action 151–2

harassment, uncovering 173

short-term absence 151–2, 168–77

training line managers 177–8

underlying causes of absence 171–2

review dates, rehabilitation 103–4

reviewing, triggers for action155

rigorous notification procedures, short-term absence 164–7

risk assessments 42

rehabilitation 104

risk reduction, occupational health professionals 62

roles

defining 33–9

line managers 34–5, 36–7, 71–3

management 34–9, 71–3

personnel function 37–8

senior managers 34–6

strategy 2–3

screening, pre-employment 62–3, 178–9

senior managers

roles 34–6

severity of absence 46

short-term absence 145–87

action short of dismissal 148–55, 162–3

advice, medical 159–60

AWOL, employee going 166

causes 145–6

disability-related 157–60

disciplinary action 148–67

dismissals 25–6, 155–62, 166–7

eradicating unnecessary 146–7

formal action 148–67

formalities, procedural 160–4

harassment, uncovering 173

medical advice 159–60

notification procedures 164–7

procedural formalities 160–4

record-keeping 157–9

return to work interviews 151–2, 168–78

spot checks 178

strategy 6

underlying causes of absence
171–2
unnecessary 146–7
wilful misconduct 153
sick notes *see* medical certificates
sick pay *see* company sick pay;
statutory sick pay
signing off *see* medical certificates
Society of Occupational Medicine
(SOM) 68
SOM *see* Society of Occupational
Medicine
spot checks, employees 55, 178
SSP *see* statutory sick pay
statutory procedural rules
accompanied, right to be 31,
163–4
compliance 30, 106–7
discipline 28
dismissal 28
employees' obligations 29–30
employer requirements 29
grievance 28
legal issues 27–32
long-term absence 104–11
penalties, non-compliance 30
record-keeping 31
short-term absence 160–4
statutory sick pay (SSP)
notification procedures 168
qualification for 120–1
withholding 94, 120–1, 124, 168
strategy 1–14
inform/involve workforce 4
priorities 3–4

rehabilitation 5–6
roles 2–3
short-term absence 6
support 4–5
training 6
stress, case study 136–42
surveillance 54–5

tax liability, paying for treatment
92–3
team competition 184
terms and conditions, rehabilitation
101–2
trade unions
rehabilitation 131
sick pay 131
training
management 177–8
rehabilitation 89
return to work interviews 177–8
strategy 6
transport, rehabilitation 89
treatment
medical, paying for 90–3
triggers
absolute 154–6
comparative 154–6
formal action 154–6
reviews 155

underlying causes of absence, return
to work interviews 171–2
unfair dismissal
avoiding, long-term absence
104–11

avoiding, short-term absence
153–64
DDA 16
principles 24–32
unnecessary short-term absence,
eradicating 146–7

visiting workplace, employees 87

waiting lists, NHS delays 90, 130
warnings
dismissals 104–9
vs. cautions 149–51
websites
absence and labour turnover
172
AWS 67
Code of Practice 18
DEAs 66
defining disability 108
EEF Employment Guide 17, 21

Employers' Forum on Disability
69
medical certificates 116, 118,
119, 120, 121
NHS Plus 68
SOM 68
SSP 120, 121
work-related personal injury 129
WorkCare 68
wilful misconduct, short-term
absence 153
work content, rehabilitation 88
work-related personal injury 129
WorkCare 68
workplace adaptation, rehabilitation
88–9
Workplace (Health, Safety and
Welfare) Regulations (1992),
disability discrimination 24
Workstep Scheme 67
written reasons, dismissals 190